D0329371

A RENAISSANCE WOMAN

First page of the first letter of the 1539 edition of Helisenne's letters, published by Denys Janot (*detail*).

a Renaissance Woman

Helisenne's Personal and Invective Letters

Translated and edited by
MARIANNA M. MUSTACCHI
and
PAUL J. ARCHAMBAULT

SYRACUSE UNIVERSITY PRESS
1986

Copyright © 1986 by SYRACUSE UNIVERSITY PRESS
Syracuse, New York 13210

FIRST EDITION
All Rights Reserved

Papers based on portions of the Introduction were read at the Ninth Conference on Medieval Studies, the Medieval Institute, Western Michigan University; and the Fifth Interna-
tional Conference on Patristic, Mediaeval, and Renaissance Studies, sponsored by the Au-
gustinian Historical Institute, Villanova University.

MARIANNA M. MUSTACCHI is Associate Professor of French and chairs the Depart-
ment of Modern Languages at Bucknell University. PAUL J. ARCHAMBAULT is
Professor of French at Syracuse University. He is the author of *Camus' Hellenic
Sources*, and *Seven French Chroniclers* (Syracuse University Press).

We are grateful for the help offered by two institutions in the preparation of this book:
Bucknell University, whose generous support was instrumental in carrying out research, and
the American Philosophical Society, which supplied summer travel funds through the Pen-
rose Fund.

The paper used in this publication meets the minimum requirements of American National
Standard for Information Sciences—Permanence of Paper for Printed Library Materials,
ANSI Z39.48-1984. ∞

Library of Congress Cataloging-in-Publication Data

Crenne, Hélisenne de.
   A Renaissance woman.

   Translations of portions of: Les Angoisses douloureuses
qui procèdent d'amours and Les Epistres familières et
invectives.
   Bibliography: p.
   Includes index.
   1. Crenne, Hélisenne de—Translations, English.
I. Mustacchi, Marianna M. II. Archambault, Paul J.,
1937–   . III. Crenne, Hélisenne de. Épistres
familières et invectives. English. Selections. 1985.
IV. Title.
PQ1607.C65A26   1985   843'.3   85-20812
ISBN 0-8156-2347-X
ISBN 0-8156-2348 (pbk.)

Manufactured in the United States of America

CONTENTS

The INVECTIVE LETTERS of LADY
    HELISENNE de CRENNE

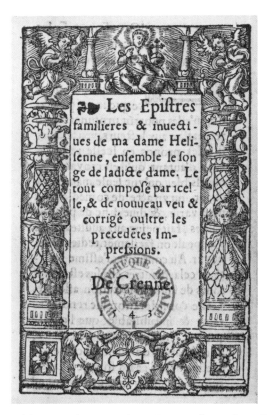

Title page of the second section of *Les Oeuvres de ma dame Helisenne*,
published by Charles Langelier in 1543.

INTRODUCTION

LIFE AND WORKS

AMONG the neglected writers of French Renaissance literature, Helisenne de Crenne is perhaps one of the most worthy of rediscovery. What little we know about her life must principally be inferred from her two major works, *Les Angoysses douloureuses qui procedent d'amours* (1538) and *Les Epistres familieres et invectives* (1539). Helisenne's real name was Marguerite de Briet. Born in the village of Abbeville, in Picardy, presumably between 1510 and 1520, Marguerite chose to publish under the pen name Helisenne, perhaps because of the name of a character in a contemporary romance. Helisenne acquired the surname de Crenne (which documents also spell Cresnes, Crasnes, and Crennenes) when she married a country squire named Philippe Fournel, seigneur de Crenne.

At least one child, Pierre, was born of the marriage. According to a document dated 9 August 1548, Pierre was receiving a pension of fifty *livres tournois* at the Collège de Navarre, in Paris, which leads one to infer that Helisenne and Philippe were married around 1530. A document of 1550 mentions a debt of forty *livres tournois* which Philippe and demoiselle Marguerite were forced to pay a baker

1

of the *faubourg* Saint Marcel: the considerable amount of the debt would indicate that the couple resided together for a while in that Parisian suburb.

If *Les Angoysses* are even partly autobiographical, as they purport to be, Helisenne's marriage to Philippe was a stormy one from the earliest years. *Les Angoysses* tells the story of a young girl named Helisenne given in marriage to a cantankerous, jealous, sadistic husband who resents his wife's beauty. Some time after marrying, the young girl falls passionately in love with a young man named Guenelic. The husband proceeds to spy on her, to lock the girl in her room, and reserves the right to enter occasionally in order to threaten or beat her. He finally imprisons her in one of his castles.

If the content of *Les Epistres familieres et invectives* is autobiographical, Helisenne and Philippe were already separated in 1539. Their separation seems to have been legally sanctioned, for a document dated 25 August 1552 mentions an annual pension of two hundred thirteen *livres tournois* made out by Marguerite de Briet, "wife of Philippe Fournel, Lord of Crasnes, separated from him as to possessions," to a certain Christophe le Manyer and his heirs, "for good and pleasant services." Now residing at Saint Germain des Prés, Helisenne had couched that document in the form of a will. She did not elaborate as to the identity of the squire whom she had chosen as her beneficiary, or the nature of the good and pleasant services for which she felt duty-bound to reward him.[1]

It would be misleading to assume that Helisenne's works are merely autobiographical in their content. As the following summary shows, Helisenne had a broad range of interests reflecting many of the intellectual currents of her day.

Les Angoysses douloureuses qui procedent d'amours

Published in Paris in 1538 by Denys Janot, this seemingly autobiographical tale combines elements of the psychological novel and of the traditional novel of chivalry. Narrated by a beautiful young girl named Helisenne, the first of its three parts tells how she was married in her eleventh year to an older man, then fell hopelessly in love with a gallant young admirer. The unhappy consequences of this situation are related in parts two and three. The author here foregoes the subtle analyses of part one for the more heavy-footed techniques of medieval romance. Highly popular in Helisenne's time—they had been printed eight times by 1560—*Les Angoysses* have not been reprinted in their entirety since then. Two separate critical editions of part one appeared in 1968, both in Paris: one by Paule Demats, at Les Belles Lettres; the other by Jérôme Vercruysse, at Lettres Modernes (Minard).

Les Epistres familieres et invectives

Written in prose with no connecting materials, these eighteen letters were published by Denys Janot in 1539. Like the preceding work, *Les Epistres* are a reconstruction of the main facts surrounding Helisenne's marriage, her ill-fated love, her publication of *Les Angoysses*, and her husband's hostility to the book's publication. *Les Epistres* had been through eight printings by 1560, but they have never been printed since. The present English translation is the first in any language.

Le Songe de madame Helisenne, composé par ladicte Dame, la consideration duquel est apte à instiguer toutes personnes de s'aliener de vice et s'approcher de vertu

In this dream allegory Helisenne witnesses a debate led by Reason, Charity, and Chastity on one side, and Sensuality and Shame on the other. The allegorical structure of *Le Songe* owes much to medieval predecessors such as *Le Roman de la rose* and Christine de Pisan's *Le Livre de la cité des dames*, but the pastoral setting and the presence of divinities like Venus, Cupid and Minerva bring back classical reminiscences (such as the Judgment of Paris as Helisenne might have read it in the contemporary romance by Jean Lemaire de Belges, *Illustrations de Gaule*). A further link to classical antiquity is Helisenne's claim that her *Songe* was inspired by the *Somnium Scipionis*, the last book of Cicero's *De Republica*, which was highly popular in Helisenne's time and usually printed, both in Latin and in French translation, as a separate treatise. Helisenne's *Songe* purports to imitate the Ciceronian treatise on the "machine of the world and immortality of the soul," but it is in fact the account of a renunciation of sexual passion for a life guided by Reason, Charity, and Chastity. The debate between the allegorical figures raises classical comparisons as to the moral makeup of men and women. Reason cites arguments from Saint Paul, Saint Augustine, and Saint Thomas to conclude that Woman is not a cause of sin but the reason for Man's glory. Denys Janot published *Le Songe* the first time in 1540, reprinted it in 1541, then combined it with *Les Angoysses* and *Les Epistres* in *Les Oeuvres de ma dame Helisenne*, which were printed seven times between 1543 and 1560.

Les quatre premiers livres des Eneydes du treselegant poete Virgile, traduictz de latin en prose Françoyse par ma dame Helisenne, à la traduction desquelz y a pluralité de propos qui par maniere de phrase y sont adjoustez: ce que beaucoup sert à l'elucidation et decoration desdict livres,

dirigez à tresillustre et tresauguste Prince Françoys,
premier de ce nom invictissime Roy de France

Helisenne's last known work was printed only once, by
Denys Janot in 1541. It appeared in a larger format than
Les Angoysses of 1538 or *Les Epistres* of 1539 (eight by
ten inches as against three by six inches), on paper of
higher quality, and with many woodcut illustrations. The
care and luxury surrounding this edition are no doubt due
to the exalted state of the king to whom it is dedicated.
This work, Helisenne's only published translation, is both
traditional and innovative in its approach. The *Aeneid* was
by no means a novel choice for a translator. Virgil had
been studied without interruption since antiquity and he
was no less popular in the Middle Ages than at the time of
the Renaissance. Indeed, the Virgil whose biography Helisenne relates in the short preamble is the medieval, legend-
ary Virgil, credited with having performed many acts of
necromancy.[2] True to medieval practice, Helisenne adds
explicative glosses in the margins of her translation, and
embellishments without indicating her deviation from the
original. In sections where she feels that Virgil's account is
insufficient (in the account of Achilles' slaying of Hector,
for example, in Book II), she adds several pages of narrative excerpted from other versions. Helisenne's translation
of the first four books of the *Aeneid* may still be steeped in
medieval tradition, but it is the first known unabridged
translation of those books in French prose.[3]

In *Les Epistres familieres et invectives* Helisenne attempts what had perhaps never been attempted before in
French literature, the progressive construction of a story
through letters, without the use of connective materials.
The two groups of letters, thirteen personal and five invec-

tive, differ sharply in tone. The first eight personal letters bring advice and consolation to friends and colleagues. Writing as a young but disillusioned married woman, Helisenne tells an abbess that she is seriously attracted to life in a convent from which she has just returned (Letter one); she declines a relative's invitation to a wedding, preferring to stay with her aging and ailing mother (Letter two); she instructs a friend whose character has been smeared to be patient and remember the story of the chaste Suzanna, a model of vilified innocence (Letter three); she exhorts Cornelio, a friend who has been unjustly banished from court, to remember the wisdom of Socrates and the patience of Cassiodorus (Letter four); she tries to convince a certain Galazia to be reasonable and end her illicit love affair (Letter five); she consoles Meliadus and Guisnor, the former for having lost some of his wealth (Letter six); the latter for having lost a beloved wife (Letter seven); she upbraids Clarissa for loving a man whom her parents find an unacceptable partner and advises her to marry according to her parents' wishes (Letter eight).

The ninth personal letter brings a change of tone and style. Helisenne again writes Clarissa, this time advising her to persist in hiding her illicit love from her parents if she is unable to suppress her passion. In Letter ten she admits to Galazia that she herself is in love with a man not her husband, and apologizes for having seemed self-righteous in her previous letters. Letter eleven, again sent to Galazia, describes the state of depression into which Helisenne has fallen because of ugly rumors which have arisen over her illicit love affair. In Letter twelve, a Ciceronian encomium on friendship, Helisenne begs Quezinstra to help her obtain release from the captivity into which her husband has thrown her. Letter thirteen, the last of the "familiar" group, is a coded message to her lover telling him of all the suffering she has endured for him and is willing to endure for him still.

The first three of Helisenne's invective letters deal with responses to her husband's accusations and show her at the peak of her literary form. In the first letter Helisenne lists the accusations which her husband has levelled against her, then proceeds to refute them systematically. She ridicules her husband's claim that she has published *Les Angoysses* in order to commemorate "an indecent and lascivious love," demonstrates the absurdity of his thinking that literature is necessarily a record of personal experience, and warns him of the danger of trying to improve his reputation by destroying hers.

The second invective letter is the husband's reply, which Helisenne writes in her most vituperative hand. He tells her that she would have to die many times before incurring a sufficient punishment for her crime of infidelity, and that he needs no detractors to ruin her reputation, having witnessed her conduct at first hand. He then proceeds to extend the accusation of faithlessness to all of womankind, cites the example of Socrates, laments the fate of great heroes who have been betrayed by the women they loved, and concludes that Woman is Man's most dangerous enemy.

Helisenne refutes these accusations in the third invective, arguing that if women were as "unfaithful, inconstant, fraudulent, and deceitful" as her husband says they are, no one would ever dare venture into the state of marriage. Socrates' ideas on marriage, she continues, were perhaps somewhat biased because of his unfortunate marriage to a shrew. Quoting extensively from the classics, the Church Fathers and the Scriptures, Helisenne refutes the accusation that women's use of ornaments and makeup is proof that they are lustful and that women are to be blamed if men succumb to their physical charms.

The fourth and fifth invectives deal with a woman's right to pursue literary studies. Letter four paises the sophisticated populace of the "noble Parisian city," who welcome and encourage a woman's literary endeavours and whose editors and literary public are the most enlightened in the world; Letter five is directed against the benighted residents of a small city, perhaps Helisenne's native Abbeville, who have criticized her for publishing *Les Angoysses* and in so doing have justified Helisenne's choice of Paris as the only city wherein to pursue her literary career.

THE EPISTOLARY TRADITION

Helisenne brought to her letters a great originality of tone, color, content, and style; but any series of letters called "familiar" and "invective" could not be unmindful of a past literary tradition. The very title *Les Epistres familieres* was meant to be read with its root Latin meaning and to call to mind Cicero's *Epistolae ad familiares*. The similarities, both thematic and stylistic, are evident, though they are not so close as to indicate that Helisenne directly and systematically copied from Cicero's letters. Some of Helisenne's letters indicate that she might have used Cicero as a model though not necessarily as a direct source. For example her letters of consolation to Cornelio (four) and Meliadus (six), in which she raises such notions as adversity, banishment, and betrayal, may have been inspired by a contemporary French translation of Cicero's *Epistres familières*,[4] or by a manual on techniques of letter writing entitled *Le Grand et vray art de pleine réthorique*, which was available in Helisenne's time.[5]

Helisenne's encomium on friendship (Letter twelve) naturally reminds one of Cicero's *De Amicitia* and is stylistically close to a French translation of that treatise published by Denys Janot in 1539, entitled *Livre de l'amytie*. Her letter to Guisnor (seven) beseeching him not to grieve excessively over the death of his young wife is a striking evocation of the famous letter written to Cicero after the death of his daughter Tullia by his friend Servius Sulpicius Rufus.

Invective letters were also an ancient classical genre revived during the age of humanism. Christine de Pisan is credited for using the word "invective," as Petrarch had done some years before. Helisenne could have come across the word in the aforementioned manual of epistolary style published in 1535 by Denys Janot, Pierre Fabri's *Le Grant et vray art de pleine rethorique utille proffitable et necessaire a toutes gens qui desirent a bien elegantement parler et escripre*, one section of which deals with instructions for writing "lettres missives de invective." It is clear, moreover, that Helisenne is conscious of the "Heroides" tradition in writing the invective letters: she had surely read some or all of Ovid's twenty-one *Heroides*, most of which are long complaints in verse attributed to famous mythological women and intended for their unfaithful lovers. A highly popular work in Helisenne's time, the *Heroides* were frequently translated into French. One of these translations, *Les xxi epistres*, was published by Denys Janot in 1539.[6]

Les Epistres familieres et invectives also pursue a more recent epistolary tradition. Since the fourteenth century, long, elegant private letters were being written, circulated, and published with a reading public in mind. Petrarch (1304–74) had been one of the first to reinstate the long continuity of letter writing dating back to antiquity. Italian humanists after him wrote and collected their own letters, and at the same time carefully polished and revised them. The letters of men such as Bruni, Poggio, Guarini, and Pietro Aretino were not only intended for their addressees but meant to be enjoyed and shown around as examples of beautifully written missives.

Besides personal correspondence, many tales and collections of tales from the fourteenth and fifteenth centuries
were cast in an epistolary mold, or relied on letters inter-
spersed with sections of narrative to further the plot. Boccaccio's love tale, *Fiammetta*, while it is called an elegy, is a
tale told in letter form by the eponymous heroine to all
women in love. Ovidian in conception and style, it is very
similar to Phyllis' letter to Demophon (*Heroides*, II) containing, in the words of the Prologue, "the sighs, the tears
and prolonged miseries of an enamoured young Gentle-
woman forsaken of her lover, who doth not conceive this
very same to be set forth as a sovereign example, and sole
instruction of you all." The most popular of Boccaccio's
works after the *Decameron*, *Fiammetta* had a perceptible
influence on Helisenne's first work;[7] *Les Angoysses* contains several letters written by the heroine to her lover,
which play an important role in the plot's development.

Helisenne's use of letters in *Les Angoysses*, and even
more in *Les Epistres*, was by no means the first example of
the epistolary tradition in French literature. Letters and letter collections as well as tales and poems in epistolary form
had appeared well before the 1530s. From the Provençal
Salut d'Amours to the epistolary poems of Charles
d'Orléans, the epistolary style was already flourishing in
French literature during the medieval period. Among other
illustrious predecessors in the use of the epistolary genre,
one might mention Guillaume de Machaut's *Confort
d'ami* (1356), Froissart's *Espinette amoureuse* (1372) and
Prison amoureuse (1373), Christine de Pisan's *Epistre au
dieu d'amours* (1399) and *Le Livre du duc des vrais amans*
(1404), Charles d'Orléans' *Le Poème de la prison* (ca.
1440), and Octavien de Saint Gelais' translation of Ovid's
Heroides into French prose (1493).

To consider *Les Epistres familieres et invectives* as

merely another moment in the long history of the epistolary genre would no doubt be an insufficient reason to
translate them into English for the benefit of twentieth-
century readers. Indeed, if the collection had ceased with
the ninth *Epistre familiere*, Helisenne's epistolary work
would perhaps seem of little genuine interest, for up to that
point in the sequence the letters are filled with many of the
conventional ideas and tropes so familiar to readers of Cicero's letters: consolations to friends over the loss of a beloved spouse, over a banishment from court, over the loss
of possessions; above all, exhortations to female friends to
resist sexual passion which "destroys the soul."

These themes are familiar enough to anyone acquainted with the Stoic and Christian moral traditions.
Helisenne does seem at times to be writing as if Cicero,
Saint Augustine or Saint Jerome were echoing in her ears.
But there is an innovative, personal twist to her writing
starting with Letter nine of *Les Epistres familieres*. The letters following tell the fascinating story of the collapse of
Helisenne's own inner defenses. Her somewhat smug defi-
nitions of life culled from literary and social conventions
and the ritual language of religion seem to clash here with
an unexpected firsthand experience of illicit love. Her defenses break down and the results are both innovative for
her and beneficial for her literary style. Rather than destroy her as she had feared, her illicit passion fills her with
a new awareness, once she has traversed the slough of depression and self-hatred. From the tenth *Epistre familiere*
to the thirteenth, Helisenne's marmorean prose becomes
both vibrant and vivacious. Even her once-bookish classical references begin to throb with a new vitality, as when
she learns that her lover has left the city: "Apollo himself
must not have felt more helpless when they told him that
the child Hyacinthus was dying." Gone are the pious tru-

isms of Letters one to nine, gone the persistent defensive-
ness of intellect and will toward passion, the morbid fear
of losing control and falling into chaos. Helisenne's literary reenactment of a soul in conflict evolves remarkably
with the last four personal letters. Rather than represent
passion as a struggle between artificially established
"higher" and "lower " orders of the soul, she admits to
herself that an integration of reason and passion is not
only viable but necessary if the conventional wisdom that
she has inherited is to have any meaning for her life. She
learns not to mistake sententiousness for wisdom and proceeds to a reevaluation of herself. *Les Epistres familieres*
can be read as the account of that reevaluation, and in this
regard they are worthy of being considered as forming an
epistolary novel.

Like *Les Epistres familieres, Les Epistres invectives*
point to a conflict between theory and experience. The personal letters had rejected abstract reasoning for experience; the invective letters tell the story of a conflict between a husband's abstract accusations and his wife's
concrete refutations. The subject of this collection is the
moral integrity of womankind; in the second invective,
Helisenne makes her husband the spokesman for abstract,
derivative, bookish reasoning about women when she has
him write:

> There have been many warnings against marriage in litera-
> ture; but those who have written these things have not
> demonstrated as much pain, toil, and trouble in all their
> writings as a single woman has provided her husband in a
> single day. O how the wise man should think twice before
> submitting with a woman to the connubial bond! For he
> must open his heart wide and accept all that customarily
> comes with her. Take Socrates: he tolerated so much grief
> from Xanthippe and with so much patience, he saw in
> women such malice that once, being asked what he

thought of women, he said they reminded him of a tree named Adelfa—beautiful to look at but full of poison.

The husband's letter is, of course, Helisenne's creation, acting as a foil so as to give her riposte greater relief: "If you say that Socrates railed against all women generically [*generalement*] you must remember that he himself belonged to the category [*condition*] of henpecked husbands" (Invective three).

Helisenne is here demonstrating, no doubt with tongue in cheek, that a woman too can quote scholastic categories to her purpose. The route she adopts to counter the male argument is clever: rather than attempt to refute a general assertion that is based on a single instance by citing a contrary example, she argues that the single example (Socrates) belongs to a category (henpecked husbands) which in fact disqualifies him from making an objective assertion. Helisenne also makes another point that is less significant for its literary interest than for its concrete truth: the list of bad women drawn from literature simply does not exhaust the available categories of womankind. No one better understood this than King Solomon, in whose Book of Wisdom many warnings are to be found against bad women, "but you must understand that this is a marvellous way of promoting good women" (Invective three).

Helisenne's *Les Epistres invectives* should be read as a dialogue between two voices, one the voice of abstract antifeminism, sustained by many centuries of misogynic commentary, and the gentler voice of experience and good sense, which can draw equal sustenance from that same tradition. If *Les Epistres familieres* are an account of the victory of life over abstract reasoning, *Les Epistres invectives* are a response—reasoned, dignified, hurt, ironic, and playful by turns—to a long tradition of classical and Judeo-Christian antifeminism.

HELISENNE AND HER TIME

The preceding overview of Helisenne's life, works, and literary influences gives evidence of her genuine interest in
the intellectual issues of her time and raises questions as to
her background and milieu. We are almost completely
without information about her schooling or her literary
education. It was not an anomaly around 1530 that a
woman of middle-class background from Picardy, able to
travel to Paris and even to live in the capital for extensive
periods of time, should have had an impressive education
in literature and the arts. It is useful to recall that Picardy
in the sixteenth century was by no means an economic or
cultural desert. The town of Noyon was the cradle of John
Calvin in 1509; and Marguerite de Briet's home town of
Abbeville could lay claim to printing the first French translation of Saint Augustine's *De ciuitate Dei*, that of Raoul
de Presles in 1486, which might be the translation cited by
Helisenne on several occasions in *Les Epistres*.

Helisenne may have been taught by tutors, as many
young girls of her milieu were in those days, and was perhaps never affiliated with a formal institution of learning,
whether in her early years, or later as a writer. She does not
seem to have had extensive contacts at the French court.
She was not indifferent to court patronage, as is made clear
by the fulsome praise she bestows on Marguerite de
Navarre (Invective four) and by her dedicating her translation of the *Aeneid* to the "invincible" King Francis I; but
we have no evidence that she ever succeeded in obtaining
Valois favors.[8]

During her short but intense period of publication
(September 1538–March 1541), Helisenne's patron and
mentor, assuming she had one at all, could have been
Denys Janot. Bookseller and printer, Denys Janot was ac-
tive in Paris "at the sign of Saint John the Baptist, rue

Neuve Notre Dame," from 1529, the year he took over his
father's publishing business, until his death in 1544. A
glance at the catalogue of books which he printed permits
several assumptions about his tastes and preferences.[9] He
published a broad variety of texts, including anatomical
treatises by Galen, but he seems to have concentrated on
works of literary value representing the major intellectual
concerns of his time. That tendency seems to have grown
with the years. A majority of the texts published by Janot
were in French. Only a few were in Latin, and since Janot
abandoned Gothic for Roman typography one can assume
he was aiming at a general reading public. Janot took ever
increasing care in the layout and use of woodcut illustrations; his high level of artistry, combined with his predilec-
tion for humanistic subjects, won him the distinction of being named "imprimeur du roy en langue française" in
1543. This honor gave him greater freedom in publishing
and expressed the king's desire that books printed in
French should receive as much care as books printed in
Greek and Latin.

An examination of Denys Janot's catalogue reveals
that Helisenne's four books, which he printed between
1538 and 1541, fit into his general publication scheme.
Novels of thwarted love, such as Helisenne's *Les Angoysses*, abound: *La deplourable fin de Flamecte*, by Jean
de Flores, translated by Maurice Scève (Omont 28, 64;
Rawles 50); the *Dialogue très élégant intitulé le Peregrin*, by Giacomo Caviceo, translated by François d'Assy
(Omont 119; Rawles 35); and Boccaccio's *Philocope*,
translated by Adrien Sevin (*Le Philocope de Me Jean
Bocacce*, Omont 125; Rawles 164). Denys Janot's publication of Ovid (*Les quinze livres de la métamorphose* [Rawles 105]; *Les xxi epistres d'Ovide* [Omont 53;
Rawles 50]), and Cicero (*Les oeuvres de M.T. Cicero*, including among other selections, *Les Paradoxes, Le Songe*

de Scipio [Omont 114; Rawles 91, 92, 94]; *La première*
[et seconde] partie des Epistres familieres de M.T. Cicero
[Omont 59, Rawles 63, 93]), to which Helisenne makes
reference or implicit allusions in her *Les Epistres*, allows us
to assume something further about Helisenne's formation:
not only did her works fit into Denys Janot's program of
publication, but the ready availability of these other works
in the catalogue may have given shape to Helisenne's ideas.
There is textual evidence throughout *Les Angoysses* and
Les Epistres that all of the works mentioned above were
familiar to her. Other works published by Janot raise
feminine issues with which Helisenne dealt in *Les Epistres.*
Noteworthy among them are Plutarch's *Du gouvernement*
en mariage (Rawles 42); DuPont's *Controverses des sexes*
masculin et femenin (Omont 27; Rawles 73); Cornelius
Agrippa's *Declamation de la noblesse et pre-excellence du*
sexe feminin (Omont 6; Rawles 227); La Borderie's
L'Amie de court (Omont 8, 97); and Heroët's *La parfaicte*
amye (Omont 121).

Establishing a connection between Helisenne and
Denys Janot allows one to clarify two questions about her
education and career which have remained mysterious until now. One of these has dealt with the availability of
books: how did Helisenne acquire her knowledge of classical and Christian writers and develop her awareness of humanistic issues? Unattached as she apparently was to any
institution of learning, a woman of her class could not easily accede to the book collections of monasteries and libraries. If we assume that she was rich enough to have a library of her own, then her association with Denys Janot
provided the source and framework she needed in order to
function. We might, moreover, understand the unusually
rapid rate of her literary output during the years 1538–41
if we assume that Denys Janot not only encouraged but
commissioned her work. We know that the immediate ac-

claim of *Les Angoysses* by the Parisian literary public led Denys Janot to make an explicit request for exclusive publication rights, as the printer's foreword in *Les Epistres* makes clear; there is every reason to believe, therefore, that Janot considered Helisenne's work an invaluable literary property.[10]

A second question to which Helisenne's association with Janot brings a hypothetical answer is her choice of pen name. The only other "Helisenne" ever mentioned in literature seems to be the mother of the eponymous hero of the novel *Amadis*, published by Janot in 1540. If we assume that Janot's interest in Helisenne's career was personal enough for him to suggest a pen name, then the chivalric tale of *Amadis*, though Janot did not publish it until 1540, could easily have been available to Helisenne in manuscript form in 1538.[11]

To assume that Helisenne limited her book purchases or her intellectual associations to Denys Janot would, of course, be foolish. Indeed her association with him may have provided entries into the literary world of that "noble Parisian city" which she praises so highly in Invective four. Janot's establishment was situated in the Ile de la Cité, rue Neuve Notre Dame, surrounded by other publishing houses. Like other publishers he also owned a shop in the Palais Royal, "behind the first pillar." A close examination of his catalogue reveals that he collaborated with other printers and bookdealers, and it is not always clear from his catalogue whether he is promoting a volume as its printer or serving as bookseller for another printer. A successful printer, an adept collaborator with publishers, even singled out by the king for his services, Denys Janot may well have been the mentor, promoter, and patron that Helisenne needed.

With the exception of her translation of Virgil, Helisenne's works all deal with what might today be called

women's rights: the right to a sexual and emotional life of
their own, the right to love, marriage, education, and a literary career. Helisenne was not the first woman nor alone
in her time, surely, to deal with ideas such as these; but
rarely had a woman writer expressed herself with such
a combination of passion and erudition. It is this combination of personal experience with erudition that sets
Helisenne apart from her contemporaries who participated
in the debate known as the "quarrel of women." She is
well-schooled in the traditional sense; she has read and di-
gested the same books as the humanists of her time and respects the traditional institutions (church, marriage, family); she may even grant to men the advantages they have
been claiming for generations and acknowledge assumptions made to the detriment of her sex; but while re-
maining within the boundaries, both social and cultural,
established by the masculine world, she manages to argue
her point of view. She might even turn a male argument
against itself with an appeal to the same classical and
Christian writers to sustain her assertions. Whereas
many contemporary treatises on the subject of feminine issues use blocks of erudition as so many pieces in a heavy,
colorless construction, Helisenne brings lightness and
depth to her book knowledge with personal experience
and insight.

As a defender of women and of their right to love,
marriage, education, and career, hers was not a voice in
the wilderness in the literature of the 1530s and 40s. Indeed, the "Querelle des Femmes," which had laid dormant
in much of fourteenth- and fifteenth-century literature,
had become a live issue once again. Begun in the late thirteenth century, the "Querelle des Femmes" revolved about
the issue of Woman's inherent nature in comparison to
Man's, and the status and privileges that derive from that
nature. The quarrel polarized opposite and extreme points

of view from the very start. In 1277, Jean de Meung opposed the idealized conception of Woman held by the courtly love tradition and launched a virulent attack upon the female sex in the second part of *Le Roman de la rose*, in which he described women as lascivious, deceitful, and conniving creatures. Around the early fifteenth century, Jehan de Montreuil and the humanists Gontier and Pierre Col sided with the antifeminist view of Jean de Meung. Their position drew a response from the learned and prolific Christine de Pisan (1365–1430) who, in Montreuil's opinion, "was not entirely lacking in wit, inasmuch as a woman can have any." Christine comes to the defense of ladies in many of her works, particularly the allegorical *Le Livre de la cité des dames*, where she argues effectively against the traditional accusations that women are more lascivious than men, lead men to perdition, and are the sole cause of unhappy marriages. Christine found an unexpected ally in her prestigious contemporary, Jean Gerson, an austere churchman hardly known for his feminism, but opposed to Jean de Meung's dark and "immoral" vision of women.[12]

Discontinued during much of the fifteenth century because of French political instability, the quarrel of women gathered a new momentum in the early sixteenth. The basic points at issue, whether Woman is merely an imperfect male, whether she is equal to Man in the eyes of God, whether she is physically and morally inferior to Man, whether she is more sensuous than Man, had been debated since the time of Plato and Aristotle (later Galen), and the answers provided were not usually favorable to womankind. Aristotle's reference to Woman as an "aberration of nature" found a scholastic echo in Saint Thomas' moderate view of Woman as a being inferior to Man in her capacity for virtue and subordinated to her husband in marriage.

These interlocking assumptions, which hold that Woman is less virtuous, less rational and more lascivious than Man, helped shape the stereotyped image of Woman that is found in the popular French literature of the *fabliaux*, *farces*, and *contes*, where she is inevitably depicted as deceitful, scheming, and motivated by unbounded sexual lust. Thus "justified," the notion of female inferiority underlies the literary discussions on women in the early sixteenth century. The works of this period on the question, whether written in prose or verse, in the form of a treatise, dialogue, or compilation, in Latin or French, set forth an extreme position: women are either described as superior or inferior to men; seldom is equality or parity the dominant theme. In the course of this quarrel, the same arguments are ceaselessly repeated, the same biblical quotations are adduced as evidence, the same authorities cited in support of one side or the other.

This repetitiousness of ideas, anecdotes, and examples in the literary corpus on the quarrel of women adds to the difficulty of determining just how much of that literature Helisenne was familiar with. She is clear in some of her references to classical and Christian sources on the subject, as when she explicitly mentions Saint Jerome, Saint Augustine, or Saint Thomas; these sources represent but a fraction of those she actually read. We cannot infer from either *Les Angoysses* or *Les Epistres* whether she really read *Le Roman de la rose*, or Boccaccio's *De claris mulieribus* (1375; translated into French in 1493), or Christine de Pisan's *Le Livre de la cité des dames*. Any one of these texts, as well as their common source, Ovid, might have served Helisenne in good stead. Indeed it is a curiosity of the literature on the quarrel of women that the most familiar arguments might just as easily be found in antifeminist, profeminist, or "neutral" works. For example, Jean de Meung, Boccaccio, and Christine all provide the same examples of women known for their outstanding accomplishments or virtues (Dido, Semiramis, Lucretia), or their ill-starred love (Thisbe, Medea, Oenone).

A new and largely positive development in the literature on the quarrel of women in the early sixteenth century was the appearance of Neoplatonism. As redefined by the Florentine Neoplatonist Marsilio Ficino, the concept of Neoplatonic (or Platonic) love first appeared in France in the work of the Lyonnais physician, Symphorien Champier, entitled *La Nef des dames vertueuses* (1503). Based largely on the ideas that emerge from Plato's *Symposium* as reinterpreted by Ficino, Champier's work eschews any discussion of homosexual love and makes women the sole object of men's devotion. Neoplatonism was enthusiastically received in France, largely because it was an exotic import from the cradle of all culture, Italy, while it extended the deeply imbedded French tradition of *amour courtois* in a reading public that remained addicted to chivalric romance.

In French court circles, women were acquiring a prestige and importance worthy of the great *cortegiane* of the Italian Renaissance; and the influence that women such as Anne de Bretagne or Marguerite de Navarre exerted as patronesses of the arts was bound to have an impact on literary tastes. In dedicating his work to Anne de France, Duchesse de Bourbon, and in openly referring to his work as an "invective contre les medisans des femmes," Symphorien Champier bravely took up the literary gauntlet as the champion of womankind. Combining as it did traditional materials from Boccaccio and Christine de Pisan (the compilation of outstanding women in Book I) with the innovative Neoplatonism of Book IV, Champier's work was a resounding success. Another reason for its celebrity, incidentally, may have been the fascinating second book, which is curiously overlooked by most critics. Here

Champier entertains medical and sexual questions dealing with sex and marriage. The questions, many of them drawn from Greek treatises, raise such problems as the prescribed frequency of sexual intercourse, the time of day or night most favorable to generation, and physical causes of sexual incompatibility.

Helisenne's conception of love is in many respects Neoplatonic, like Champier's;[13] there is no evidence, however, that she had read or even knew of Champier's work. Nor, for that matter, are we certain that she had read Jean Tixier's profeminist manual entitled *De memorabilibus et claris mulieribus* (1521), a Latin compilation of several works which includes a catalogue of more than two hundred outstanding women. There is a better chance of her having read the most violent diatribe of the first three decades of the century, written in French verse and published anonymously (the first time) at Toulouse in 1534: Gratien DuPont's *Controverses des sexes masculin et femenin.*

The title should not mislead. Far from the balanced confrontation of arguments that it purports to be, the book is a unilateral attack against women, vulgar and tasteless to the modern reader, but not empty of sarcasm and even of what might have passed for humor. The *Controverses* were immensely popular and enjoyed several reprintings within a few years after their appearance; one of these editions was printed by Denys Janot (Book I, 1536; Books II-III, 1539). Given the availability of this work it is difficult not to assume that Helisenne was familiar with it. The rapier-like irony of her best invective letters (especially two and three) may owe much to the heavy-footed sarcasms of one Gratien DuPont.

Another work that Helisenne unquestionably read and generously borrowed from was Cornelius Agrippa's *De nobilitate et praecellentia feminei sexus.*[14] Written in 1509 (for Marguerite of Austria, the sister of Emperor

Charles V), but not published until 1529, Agrippa's work was well received and widely read throughout the century. A year after its publication, it appeared in a French prose translation. Several editions followed closely upon it, including one by Janot (listed as undated).

The treatise is remarkable for several reasons: Agrippa, like Champier, espouses the cause of Neoplatonism and emphasizes the importance of feminine beauty. "The duty of Justice," he argues, "compels us to love woman, respect her, honor her for she is the Queen of all creatures, the perfection, ornament and glory of creation. Woman's body is the most admirable and best arranged thing [in all creation]." Furthermore, although Agrippa reverts to the time-honored tradition of using Biblical and ancient authorities to support his arguments in favor of women, he shows ingenuity in his use of the Bible to prove the excellence of womankind. Most important, he turns away from bookish "evidence" to the real world and gives us a concrete description of the economic and social conditions of the women of his time:

> Indeed, hardly is a woman born than she is held captive in the house, without her being occupied with anything solid or serious; and as if she were incapable of anything greater, she is compelled to make of her needle and thread her sole occupation. When she attains the age of puberty, she is placed under the harsh dominion of a husband, or shut up in a monastery for the rest of her life. The laws prevent her from holding any public office. However intelligent she might be, she is not allowed to speak at the bar, she is granted no jurisdiction, no right of arbitration, of adoption, of opposition; she cannot be hired as a tutor or nurse for children; she cannot concern herself with wills or criminal affairs. She is denied the right to preach, though Scripture says: "Your daughters shall prophecy . . ." But the most recent legislators have been far different from the ear-

lier ones; they have considered women as quite inferior to
men. . . . It is not the laws of nature nor those of the Creator, and even less those of Reason which hold them in
such bondage, but a deadly education, an unhappy lot, an
unfair destiny which condemns them to this condition.[15]

Helisenne's readings may have exposed her to other
views as liberal as this one; but it is understandably Cornelius Agrippa's treatise *De nobilitate* that she drew upon
most heavily in order to sustain her own arguments and to
confirm her own experience. In refuting her husband's accusation (Invective four) that women are "unfaithful, inconsistent, fraudulent, and deceptive," she draws upon
Agrippa's list of virtuous married women, arguing that a
woman can accomplish significant deeds and be beautiful
and attractive to men, without being considered lascivious
and unfaithful. When she expresses her belief that women
should be educated and allowed to turn to literary pursuits, she turns to Agrippa's list of learned women: Zenobia, Deborah, Athalia, *et al.* When she denies that "women
are rough and benighted people whose only pastime
should be to spin, since they are incapable of writing well"
(Invective four), she once again combines Agrippa's list of
learned women with her personal experience, stressing
that women should be allowed to turn to literary pursuits
if their marital hopes have failed them.

Helisenne's invective letters thus stand at the very
center of the debate on the status of women as it was being
conducted around 1540. As the expression of deep convic-
tion and of the intensely felt emotions and frustrations of
her married life, they differ from many treatises of that
time which merely repeat bookish arguments. Hers was a
passion felt at first hand, and the vividness of that passion
instills in these letters an unmistakable, almost disquieting
ring of life. Helisenne's articulate defense of womankind

endows her work with a resonance that far transcends its own time.

HELISENNE'S LANGUAGE

In 1555, François de Billon could write that Picardy was proud of "the marvellous wit of her daughter Helisenne, whose compositions are so often in the hands of Frenchmen delighting in prose that nothing further need be said." The many editions of Helisenne's works between 1538 and 1560 were proof of her great popularity during her lifetime and lent credibility to de Billon's taunting assertion that the craftsman's crown is the work itself: "L'Oeuvre couronne l'Ouvrière."[16] Contemporaries were not unanimous, however, in their praise of Helisenne's craft: there must have been some who agreed with Etienne Pasquier's criticism of her "redundance latinicome," her abuse of elaborate periods and multisyllabic latinisms.[17] The 1550 edition of her works was revised by Claude Colet, patently in response to a request from readers that he "render into our own familiar language the obscure words that are too close to Latin." Even at the height of her literary fame Helisenne was perceived by many readers as an arcane and difficult writer.[18]

At its worst moments her prose is convoluted and euphuistic and leaves us with an unpleasant sense of oversaturation.[19] Her innumerable repetitions, citations of ancient authors, and lengthy exempla are more cumbersome than ornamental. Some of her sentences are so complex as to seem ungrammatical and to obscure their main point. Constant enumeration, repetition, and hyperbole inflate her phrasing and weaken her arguments. Hers is an almost compulsive inclination toward binary turns of phrase: syn-

onyms are coupled for emphasis ("croyable et concessible
. . . varié et diversifié . . . tedier et ennuyer"); qualifying adjectives are often implied in the noun they qualify
("téméraire hardiesse . . . acerbe regret . . . bonne exem-
plarité"), and seem superfluously added so as to maintain
a binary rhythm ("les fréquentes abstinences, la virginalle
continence, les sobres paroles, l'espargné regard, la continue demeure solitaire, la dispersée charité . . . l'aspre pén-
itence, l'extreme diligence . . . la souveraine pacience").

Helisenne's typical periodic sentence consists of one
or several main clauses, connected by conjunctions such as
et, si, puis, parquoy, with a variety of relative, concessive,
temporal, or causal clauses imbricated or imbedded into
them. Helisenne's imbedded sentences are not necessarily
the most obscure, however, and they frequently convey a
pleasant sense of rhythm and symmetry, as in the following illustration, where she sets out a long, rhythmic period,
almost as if to calm the inner agitation that has been created by a previous hypothesis:

1. J'ay quelque fois conjecturé [*main clause*]
A. que la distance des lieux t'eussent faicte immemorative
   de l'amytié precedente [*noun clause; a note of agitation
   is introduced by this hypothesis; the following periodic
   sentence provides a calming response*].
   1. Puis aprés [A] j'estimoye estre impossible [*first main
      clause*],
   A. me recordant de l'anticque coustume de conversation
      familière entre nous [*first participial clause, conveying
      a sense of relaxed "breathing"*],
   B. que tu eusse la si invétérée amytié en oblivion convertye
      [*first noun clause*],
   2. parquoy ceste fantasie sequestrée, à une aultre donnait
      lieu [*second main clause*],
   3. et estimois [*third main clause*]

C. que fortune par sa variable mutabilité t'eust fait suc-
comber en quelque sinistre accident, ou de passion de
l'ame, ou d'indisposition corporelle [*second noun
clause, symmetrical with B and almost twice as long,
setting the "B hypothesis" to flight*]

4. et [D] avoye une timeur accumulée, avec ung affec-
tueulx desir d'avoir de toy certaine science [*fourth and
final main clause*]

D. m'arrestant plus en ces ultimes imaginations, qu'en
nulle autre [*second participial clause, symmetrical with
A*].[20]

Helisenne's imbedded periods convey not merely an
occasional sense of symmetry, but the complexity of the
emotions afflicting her and their quick succession in her
consciousness. The most effective moment in the following
illustration does not reside in the comparison drawn from
Ovid, but in the almost breathless succession of mental
states which follow each other hypotactically:

> l'on m'annonca que le mien amy s'estoit absenté de la cité,
> moins ne me fut ce rapport ennuyeux, que fut à l'élargiteur
> de celeste lumiere Apollo, quand il vit ne pouvoir obvier au
> mortel inconvenient de l'enfant Hyacinthus./ Et estant ainsi
> de cruelle amaritude agitée,/ me convenoit pour la conver-
> sation d'honnesteté dissimuler:/ et avec ce j'avoye timeur
> de faire indice à jalousie,/ dont procedoit l'occasion de mon
> mal,/ parquoy si vehement estoit ma peine/ que facilement
> eust esté apte à faire du corps et de l'ame separation,/sinon
> que les nocturnes tenebres m'estoient propices/ pour
> donner lieu à quelzqu'uns de mes desirs,/ qui estoit de me
> retrouver seule.[21]

Helisenne's ability to juxtapose emotional states in
long hypotactical sentences, thereby revealing delicate
shadings of feeling, is one of the most pleasing features of
her writing. Other passages which are equally effective for

today's reader are those which were least intended to be "literary." As is so often the case with documents, whether read for historical content or literary craft, the writer is most informative when caught off guard. The following illustration, which is entirely free of rhetorical effects, describes the arrival of a lady at Helisenne's château bearing news of a maligned friend. These charming scenes from everyday life file past us like a succession of tapestries or manuscript illuminations:

> à tous mes serviteurs domestiques, ay donné expresse commission, d'avoir sollicitude, pour scavoir à ceulx qui journellement de ta region surviennent en nostre cité, s'ilz avoient de toy congnoissance. Cette inquisition estoit à eulx tresfacile à faire, pource que le vulgaire et plus commun chemin est assez proche de nostre chasteau, et à raison de cela comme survint quelque fois une dame, tant de noblesse que de beaulté et honnesteté accompaignée. Laquelle, après avoir esté de mes gens avec reverence et humilité interroguée, declaira avoir de ton estat entiere certitude, pour estre de toy amye familiere et domesticque. Et incontinent qu'advertie en fuz, allant au devant d'elle, gracieusement la saluay, et apres qu'ung doulx et begnin salut elle m'eust rendu, tresinstamment luy suppliay de se venir en nostre chasteau refociler. A quoy la modeste dame voluntairement se consentit, et depuis qu'opulentement à la refection eusmes esté servies, particulièrement de ta prospérité je m'enquis.[22]

In moments of intimacy like this one, we seem to stand at the heart of sixteenth-century life. Helisenne's literary qualities, like her faults, were, in sum, those of her time. Hers was not the plethoric genius of Rabelais, but then her verbal excesses were never so montrous. What she shares with Rabelais and other writers of the first half of her century is a sense of enthusiasm and dismay at the rediscovery of ancient texts, like children unprepared happening upon a treasure trove out of the Arabian nights. Who could face this embarrassment of riches without some sense of hyperbole, or withstand such heady spirits without some sense of giddiness? A "faithful" rendering of Helisenne's letters into English would in a strict sense require a master of sixteenth-century manneristic prose—a John Lyly, let us say, or a convincing imitator. The present translation, which, incidentally, is the first of any of Helisenne's works into any other language, has not attempted to imitate the convoluted syntax, the ornate Latinisms, and the many periphrases of the original. Our rendition has not, however, eschewed each and every one of Helisenne's rhetorical flourishes, particularly in the Invective Letters where such flourishes are an unmistakable sign of her vivacity. In our attempt at a standard English translation of *Les Epistres familieres et invectives* we have frequently simplified Helisenne's syntax and shortened many of her long periodic sentences. We have not, however, wished to stray from the original to the point of losing its flavor. No words or concepts were ever added to Helisenne's own. Only occasionally—in a long enumeration of adjectives, for example—have words been omitted. If our translation conveys the impression that this learned and aristocratic Renaissance writer was also a vibrant, sensitive, even passionate woman, it will not have failed in its purpose.

NOTES TO THE INTRODUCTION

1. Biographical information on Marguerite de Briet is based on little more than half a dozen documents, the earliest of which is dated 1539. We know neither the date of her birth nor that of her death. One document referring to her as the wife of Philippe Fournel (26 November 1539) and another mentioning her student son (August 1548) allow us to presume that she was born around 1510 or shortly thereafter. For a

discussion of these documents, see Jérôme Vercruysse, "Hélisenne de Crenne: notes biographiques," *Studi Francesi* 31 (January–April 1967): 77–81; V.L. Saulnier, "Quelques nouveautés sur Hélisenne de Crenne," *Bulletin de l'Association G. Budé*, Quatrième Série 4 (December 1964): 459–63; for a discussion of largely non-documented biographical accounts about Helisenne circulating during the nineteenth century, see Antonio Posenti, "Helisenne de Crenne nel secolo dei romantici e la prima conquista della critica," *Francia* 13 (January–March 1975): 27–40.

2. See Paule Demats' discussion of *Les quatre premiers livres des Eneydes* in Helisenne de Crenne, *Les Angoysses douloureuses qui procedent d'amours, Première partie*, edited by P. Demats (Paris: Les Belles Lettres, 1968), pp. xl–xli.

3. There was an earlier prose version published in 1483 in Lyon, which the translator, Guillaume Leroy, rearranged considerably, expanding and abridging the text aribtrarily. The better known translation, that of Octavien de Saint Gelais (1509), was done in verse.

4. Denys Janot published a two-volume French translation of Cicero's *Epistolae ad familiares* entitled: *La première [et seconde] partie des Epistres familieres de M.T. Cicero, traduction française par Guillaume Michel, de Tours* almost contemporaneously with Helisenne's *Epistres familières et invectives*. The first volume of the translation appeared in 1537; the second was published June 20, 1539, three months before Helisenne's *Epistres*, according to S.P.J. Rawles, *Denis [sic] Janot . . . A Bibliographical Study*, 3 vols., (Ph.D. thesis: University of Warwick, 1976), I, pp. 63–64; cf. Henri Omont, *Catalogue des éditions françaises de Denys Janot, libraire parisien (1529–45)* (Paris: Société de l'histoire de Paris, 1899), p. 18. We can only conjecture as to whether the Janot edition of Cicero's *Epistres familières*, copies of which the authors have been unable to consult, was available to Helisenne at the time she wrote her own letters. Innumerable Latin editions of Cicero's *Epistolae ad familiares* had appeared earlier, one as early as 1467 in Rome (ed. Swengheym and Pannartz). The earliest Latin edition of Cicero's letters to appear in France seems to have been that of the humanist Angelus Politianus (Lyon, 1496). For a catalogue of the earliest editions of Cicero available at the Bibliothèque Nationale, see *Catalogue général des livres imprimés de la Bibliothèque Nationale* (Paris: Imprimerie Nationale, 1907), vol. XXIX (*Cicero-Cleyton*), col. 99–104.

5. Published by Pierre Sargent in 1535 and again by Denys Janot in 1539, translated anonymously and compiled by Pierre Fabri (or Lefèvre), *Le Grand et vray art de pleine réthorique utile proffitable et necessaire a toutes gens qui desirent a bien elegantement parler et escripre* sets forth elaborate rules, based on classical Latin manuals of the same genre, for the writing of letters of different types: persuasion, dissuasion, congratulations, consolation, exhortation, praise, invective, etc. Selections from Cicero's letters to or from his friends serve as unfailing illustrations; and as the following parallel citations show, Helisenne may have been inspired by the work, although she is far from transcribing it literally:

Fabri, *Le Grand et vray art.*	Helisenne, *Epistres familières.*
1) toutesfoys par l'*envie* d'un meschant *flateur* . . . (Fol. Cxxxvii, a letter of consolation from Lentulus to Cicero).	1) quelques faulx *delateurs*, stimulez de ce detestable vice d'*envie* . . . (*Ep. Fam.* 4, letter of consolation to Cornelio).
2) en brief temps tu ne soys *restitué* en tes premieres dignitez (Id.).	2) futurement tu seras *restitué* (Id.).

Perhaps more convincingly indicative of this manual's influence on Helisenne's epistolary art is the advice it gives for the writing of invective letters (fol. Cxlvi): "Quant l'on veult faire lettres missives de invective, c'est de reprendre son amy ou son ennemi de aucun crime peche ou ignorance. . . ." The manual describes a "criminal" and a "contentious" way of writing invective letters. An example of the first way is Cicero's invective oration against Catiline; an illustration of the second way is Catiline's defense of himself.

6. It seems more likely, for reasons set forth in note 9 below, that Helisenne availed herself of another translation.

7. See M.J. Baker, "*Fiammetta* and the *Angoysses douloureuses qui procedent d'amours*," *Symposium* 27, no. 4 (Winter 1973): 303–308. Baker argues that the essential difference between Boccaccio's work and Helisenne's resides in Helisenne's rejection of a sensual conception of love for a spiritualized, Neoplatonic one.

8. Among the scholars who have argued that she was received at court, the least unconvincing case was made by Hyacinthe Dusevel in *Biographies des hommes célèbres . . . du département de la Somme* (Amiens: Machart, 1835), pp. 209–11. Dusevel claimed that Louise de

Savoie, mother of King Francis I, had invited Helisenne to the royal court. Contemporary scholars, among them Vercruysse and Possenti, consider this hypothesis unfounded.

9. Janot himself issued an incomplete catalogue of his publications, amounting to one hundred sixty-three items, in 1544. It was reprinted in 1899 by Henry Omont, *Catalogue des éditions françaises de Denys Janot, libraire parisien (1529–1545),* Paris, 1899. The best recent study of Denys Janot has been written by S.P.J. Rawles, "Denis Janot: Parisian Printer and Bookseller: a Bibliographical Study" (unpublished Ph.D. thesis, University of Warwick, 1976). The numerical references to Janot's list in the text are preceded by "Omont" if they are included in Omont's catalogue, by "Rawles" if included in Rawles' study.

10. Fritz Neubert suggests the same hypothesis in "Die französischen Briefschreiber der Renaissance und ihre Verleger," *Germanisch-Romanische Monatsschrift* 49, no. 18 (1968): 349–60.

11. Paule Demats has excluded, perhaps too arbitrarily, the possibility that the *Amadis* was the basis for Marguerite's pseudonym; see the introduction to her edition of *Les Angoysses douloureuses,* p. viii.

12. The indispensable source for this phase of the "Querelle des Femmes," which includes a critical edition of large sections of the major texts, is Eric Hicks, *Le Débat sur le Roman de la Rose* (Paris: Champion, 1977).

13. The influence of Christian Neoplatonism on Helisenne is discernible throughout her major works. In *Les Angoysses,* the hero and heroine never consummate their love and expect to be united only in heaven. In *Les Epistres,* Helisenne uses such conventional Neoplatonic tropes as the soul's flight from the body's prison, and the growth and fruition of conjugal love in God (Letter seven). Explicitly Neoplatonic is her conception of passionate love, with its stress on form and symbol, and the dualistic bond between terrestrial and ideal beauty. As to Helisenne's reference to love's "madness" as a "dream full of error, folly, temerity and selfishness" (Letters five, eight, and nine), it is a literary commonplace with roots in Platonism, Stoicism, Greek tragedy, and early Patristic literature.

14. For bibliographical information, see note 63.

15. *De l'excellence,* pp. 96–98.

16. François de Billon, *Le fort inexpugnable de l'honneur du sexe féminin* (Paris, 1555), fol. 35b–36a.

17. See Etienne Pasquier, *Letters* (Paris: Langelier, 1586), fol. 52b–53a.

18. "Lettre de Claude Colet," included in Helisenne de Crenne's *Oeuvres* (Estienne Groulleau, 1550); reprinted in P. Demat's critical edition of *Les Angoysses* I, pp. 102–103.

19. For a discussion of certain stylistic features found in sixteenth-century prose narratives, including Helisenne de Crenne's, see Alexandre Lorian, *Tendances stylistiques dans la prose narrative française du XVIe siècle* (Paris: Klincksieck, 1973).

20. Personal Letter Three.

21. Personal Letter Eleven.

22. Personal Letter Three.

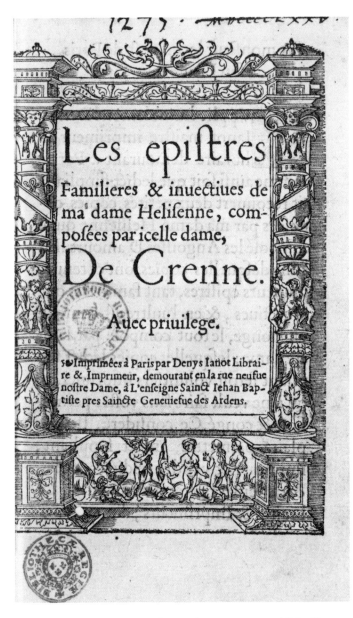

Les epiſtres

Familieres & inuectiues de
ma dame Heliſenne, com-
poſées par icelle dame,

De Crenne.

Auec priuilege.

5♣Imprimées à Paris par Denys Ianot Libraire & Imprimeur, demourant en la rue neufue
noſtre Dame, à L'enſeigne Sainct Iehan Bap-
tiſte pres Sainɾte Geneuiefue des Ardens.

Title page from the 1539 edition of *Les Epistres*, published by
Denys Janot.

The PERSONAL and
INVECTIVE LETTERS of
LADY HELISENNE DE CRENNE

TO THE PROVOST OF PARIS OR
HIS CIVIL LIEUTENANT

Oenys Janot, master printer and bookdealer, residing in Paris, addresses a humble request to the
Provost of Paris or his Civil Lieutenant, the said suppliant
having gained possession of two little volumes composed
by Lady Helisenne, the author of *Les Angoysses d'amours*.
In one of these volumes are contained several letters,
familiar and invective, and in the other a Dream, both
composed by the said Lady. These volumes the said suppliant would willingly print but cannot do so without your
leave and permission. May it please you to allow the said
suppliant to print and sell the aforesaid volumes and
forbid all other bookdealers and printers from printing, or
causing to be printed, selling or causing to be sold, the
aforesaid volumes, except those printed by the said suppliant. Infringement of this order, valid for a period of three
years, would make them liable to confiscation of the books
printed by them, and to a fine to be determined. This is to
allow the aforesaid Janot an honest reimbursement for the
expenses incurred in the printing of the aforesaid books.[1]

> Request granted for a period of two years.
> Done in Paris the 18th day of October 1539.

TO THE READER

MY BEST REASON for publishing these personal and familiar letters is that I am convinced my readers will enjoy the diversity of their contents. We all know how bored listeners can be if they are subjected to continuous chant, or how tedious it can be for spectators to see a comedy unrelieved by variety or diversity of character. In these as in other matters I believe variety is a great source of pleasure.

I am therefore convinced beyond doubt that all my gentle readers will receive the present work with a light heart, and they might even take it as evident proof of my great affection for them. I hope that my own good intentions will dispose them to increase their benevolence toward me. Prudent readers usually receive a new book with an open mind and with consideration for what the author intended; I should not have it otherwise.

Let me delay no more. But in closing this preface I shall take the advice of the sublime Plato, who tells us in his *Timaeus* that in all our works we must implore divine help. Rightly does he say so; for without divine aid it is not within Man's capacity to do anything of value. In asking for God's clemency, therefore, I beg Him to make me worthy of His assistance.[2]

La premiere epi-
stre.

ſa Epriſtre trãſmigrée par ma dame Heliſéne à vne Abbeſſe, auec laquelle elle auóit faiĉt reſidence quelque temps, & rememoiant les bons & honorables traiĉtemens, que de L'abbeſſe, enſemble des vierges veſtalles elle auoit receu, ne voulant vſer d'ingratitude , autant qu'il eſt en ſa faculté ſeſforce les remercier.

EN ayant recente memoire, O treſchere dame, des vltimes parolles, qu'a ma ſeparation d'auec toy tu pronõcas, me priant que ne feuſſe negligente d'uſer enuers toy du beneficе litteraire: affin de té manifeſt er amplemét de mes nouuelles, ſe cõſiderãt pour euirer que tu n'euſſe iuſte occaſion de me increper, pour eſtre plus

First page of the first letter of the 1539 edition of Helisenne's letters, published by Denys Janot.

FIRST PERSONAL LETTER

Lady Helisenne to an abbess, in whose convent she had spent some time as a guest. She remembers the kind hospitality she has received from the abbess and her sisters. Not wanting to appear ungrateful, she thanks them as best she can.

M Y VERY DEAR LADY, I recall your last words to me as I was taking my leave of you, begging me not to be neglectful in making use of the amenities of writing and in giving you ample news of myself; and so as to avoid giving you cause for blame, as I have been slower than your kindness toward me may have desired, I have sent you this missive to assure you that I had a pleasant trip in returning to my mother's home, where I was received so warmly that it would be difficult for me to describe to you the joy caused by my arrival, which had been so intensely expected. Several pleasant and delightful things had been prepared for me at my arrival, and I did my best to pretend to be happy at such a welcome. But please be assured beyond doubt that when I think of you and the others ladies who are ruled and governed by your discretion, a bitter sorrow fills my heart, for I feel deprived of the great privilege that was mine in participating in your devout way of life with its good examples, its assiduous worship of God, its frequent abstinences, its virginal continence, its sobriety of word and its modesty of demeanour, its solitary way of life, its well-ordered hours, its good deeds coupled with contempt for the world, its rigorous penances, its extreme diligence in devout prayers, and the sovereign patience which you exhibited in all things.

Meditating on these matters convinces me that your

life is a happy one. For in spite of bodily fatigue, you find contentment in your peace of mind, hoping for future consolation, not fearing the body's dissolution. A conscience at peace with itself knows no fear. Because of this, I had considered making my permanent home with you, had not my sense of filial duty forced my involuntary return. But bearing in mind that one cannot do as one wishes, one must do what one can. I simply must learn to bear up under this frustration. Since I am deprived of physical satisfactions, I shall have to resort to mental ones. You may therefore be assured that neither physical distance, nor passing of time, nor anything else can blot out the memory of you chaste ladies. I remember how during the time spent together each of you was so prompt in being of service to me. I cannot imagine how I could possibly satisfy this obligation for which I am beholden to each of you; but if I don't have the means to pay you back adequately, it is not for lack of fervent affection on my part. I am sure that your desire for gain is very small and that you are spared the lust of possession; but since necessity has no law, if ever you wish anything that is within my means, I herewith and forever offer and give it to you; and in ending this letter, I humbly beseech you to remember me in your holy supplications.

SECOND PERSONAL LETTER

Lady Helisenne to a relative, whom she tells of her extreme joy upon receiving a letter from her; but this happiness is not without its anxiety, for several reasons prevent her from accepting an invitation to visit.

IF EVER LETTERS or words had the strength and power to make one feel better, yours did. You can be sure that after reading you, I was supremely elated, for I felt certain that your fortune continues to be good. The best indication of this is that you tell me you have pledged in marriage your dearest only daughter to a gentleman who is rich, young, wise, handsome, and virtuous. If you reflect upon this, you shall endeavour to offer eternal praise to that Lord whose essence is present without end and knows no past nor future. Since He has made you worthy of such grace, this conjugal union causes me far more happiness than I should ever be able to express. For when I reflect over the qualities both of the aforesaid gentleman and your daughter, when I consider their prudence, wisdom, and honesty, as expressed through their words, gestures, and actions, I cannot help but think that these two beings were created in the angelic court.

In your letter, you mention the date at which you would like to have this marriage take place, and you beseech me not to miss it. What causes me some worry is that my visiting you is not within my power and does not depend upon me; the reason for this I wish to reveal to you in full so as to avoid your blaming me inadvertently and accusing me of having but little affection for my relatives. Judge for yourself after hearing the reason which prompts me to stay; I am confident beyond doubt that in your wisdom and understanding you will hold me excused. Therefore I want you to know that my mother not long ago fell gravely ill and her illness was so serious that we gave up hope for her recovery. However, the Lord was merciful toward her, so that with the help of doctors and physicians she obtained some relief from her bitter pain, which makes me think her full recovery is possible.

Given her advanced age, a complete recovery is difficult; for nothing suits her more than being comfortable, and she is inclined to resist being bled. I am sure you can see how my absence would be an inconvenience to her. She likes having me around and perhaps my presence will help to strengthen her health. I want you to know that I have preferred not to show her the letters you sent me for fear of saddening her. For although the announcement of your daughter's marriage would have caused her much pleasure, I am certain she would have felt an intense sadness along with pleasure at the thought of not being able to allow my trip to your castle. That is why I have preferred to hide this matter from her and I shall put off telling her until I feel the time is appropriate for her to know about it.

I learned from your faithful servant that your son's good spouse is pregnant and expects to be delivered around the time of the wedding celebration. The same servant told me that he was expressly charged to invite me to be present at the birth. I beg you to hold me excused and to convey my regrets.

I shall omit telling you of many other things which will be kept silent until I can be with you. Therefore I shall lay down my pen and beg the Lord to keep you happy and prosperous, and grant you a life no less durable than was that of ancient Nestor.[3]

THIRD PERSONAL LETTER

Lady Helisenne to a cousin, who is being slandered, beseeching her to bear up under this violent affliction.

I HAVE BEEN IMAGINING different reasons why you have ceased writing me as I don't know exactly what has made you so negligent. I have thought at times that the distance between us has made you forgetful of our previous friendship. Then recalling how easily we used to converse, I could not believe that you should have consigned such an old friendship to oblivion. This thought was no sooner brushed aside when another took its place, and I thought that ever-mutable fortune had made you succumb to some sinister accident, either a passion of the soul or a physical indisposition; and clinging to these suppositions, I became very fearful and so I longed to have definite news of you. I inquired about you so assiduously that I received indubitable news about your condition; a long time ago I had instructed my servants to be sure to ask those people who commute daily from your region to our city whether they had news about you. It was easy enough for them to carry out their query because the road most commonly used is located rather close to our castle. Once my servants respectfully and humbly questioned a beautiful and noble lady who said that she had definite news about you, being an intimate and close friend of yours. As soon as I was told about her, I went out to meet her, graciously greeted her, and after she had in turn graciously greeted me, I urgently begged her to come to restore herself in our castle. To which the modest lady acquiesced most willingly, and after we had been amply served in the hall I explicitly asked about your present condition.

I had no sooner begun to speak of you, when the young lady, moved by feminine compassion, began weeping. She told me of the ill luck that had befallen you some time ago, which as I understand it, was due to a malicious tongue trying to spew venom upon your modest integrity. I could not inquire further because several people arrived, and the lady wished to take her leave. After her departure, though, I was most afflicted at the thought of your problems, and I kept saying to myself: "Now you are assured of what you constantly inquired about; now you know why she has not responded. Now you fully realize that the woman from whom you hoped to have news is troubled by such violent sorrow that it has made her forget you." Then after a long lamentation I readied my trembling hand to write you again, hoping somehow to console you in this way.

I beg you to realize that the misery which friends help us bear must not be considered intolerable. Surely you are not the only one to have been persecuted by the spread of slander. Don't you know that the chaste Suzanna[4] also had her false detractors? But since the splendor of her sincerity was so bright it could not long be concealed by a false report. Her innocence was therefore cleansed and brought to light. Remember this, and it will ease your sorrow to keep in mind that they cannot contaminate your purity, however they may try, for your radiantly immaculate candour will show forth in the end. You must be certain beyond doubt that you will continue to attract the sort of praise that ennobles whoever pronounces it.

O truth, how noble you are! And with that, so strong that you always prevail. Evil and wicked gossipers are vanquished by you, and in the end perverse lies are recognized as such.

I know that for a long time you have been suffering a calamity which can only be tolerated with extreme patience. For this reason it will be most urgent and necessary for you to search within yourself to see whether this supreme virtue can be found; and having found it you must be vigilant and careful to retain it. Through patience you will understand that truth is brought to light, and if you are patient you will give clear demonstration of your sound judgement. The divine Plato was questioned once as to what signs give evidence of wisdom. He replied: "When one gives no outward sign of being irritated by an insult or puffed up by praise." Only then you might judge these persons wise. Surely this opinion by such an eminent philospher should instill in you an intense desire to resist all excessive passions, so that they will not defeat virtue. Set your mind to it. But I beg you, don't think I am writing you expecting you to be satisfied with ink and paper. I promise you that I shall come pay you a visit without fail as soon as I am able to do so. Otherwise I would not be showing you how perfect is the friendship I have for you. Anyone who comforts his friends with letters when he might have given them comfort with his presence declares himself a false friend and provides grounds for being considered a suspicious enemy in the future. If you have thought of me as a faithful friend until now, I shall give you significant proof that you must persist in this opinion of me. With this thought I bring the present letter to a close, beseeching the Prime Mover of all things to strengthen your fragile life.

FOURTH PERSONAL LETTER

Lady Helisenne to Cornelio, whom she advises to tolerate a sad situation with patience. [Cornelio has been banished from court and feels that his Prince's decision to expel him has been based on gossip and slander.]

YOUR LETTERS telling me of your anxieties trouble me greatly. I think of you in your affliction and share your pain. You may be sure, though, that the pain I suffer for your unhappiness is in no way comparable to your own, as we know that there is no comparison between hearing about someone else's persecutions and the suffering endured by that person himself. But you must believe me that close friends share their problems in common.

You tell me that your Prince has become angry with you without cause, and with no consideration for your long service has expelled you from court; and you have put youself into sad isolation, as might easily be imagined. But if you are a thoughtful, prudent man, you will take heart. Since his animosity is unfounded you have no reason to be so intensely overanxious, and to help you bear your sorrow better, remember Socrates' words during his last moments. Having been condemned to death, he saw his wife weeping and wailing, and he asked her the cause of her tears. She answered: "Don't you think that I have reason enough to be vehemently upset and persecuted seeing that you are being unjustly deprived of your life?" To which the wise philosopher answered: "My wife, I don't know what moves you to utter such things. But tell me, would the sorrow of my death be more tolerable for you if my life were being ended because of my wrongdoing?"[5] Coming from a man such as this, these words should not be forgotten, but should rather serve as an example to all those who suffer without just cause.

You say that the reason why your sorrow was increased was that friends in whom you had put your complete trust were malleable to the point of abandoning you. You shouldn't be too surprised by this. As Alain de Lille[6] has said, a person finds a great multitude of friends when he is going through a period of happiness and good fortune. But when Fortune through her instability ceases to smile upon him, then he will not find one single friend who so much as tries to be kind to him. You should put up with this annoyance, all the more so because it is so universally suffered. You say that you despair of being able to be reconciled with your Prince and that this causes you unbearable anguish. But you should consider and think about what Cassiodorus writes in his book in praise of Saint Paul,[7] where he says that the nature of evil slander is such that even when it is not opposed it succumbs under its own weight and shows its vulgarity in the sight of all. But the condition of truth is very different. It remains steadfast and firm; and the more it is opposed, the more it increases its stability and its glory. Thus we find in Holy Scripture that truth is greater than all things.

I am reminding you of this as I believe that several slandering courtiers, goaded on by the detestable vice of envy, have said something sinister about you to your Prince, in order to alienate you and completely remove you from his good graces. You will be restored to your former rank by the power of truth. But if this happy state of events occurs I beg you not to be ungrateful toward those who will have worked in favor of your reintegration. You may be sure that no matter how happy one is to be of use, one will be extremely displeased by ingratitude, which can easily make an enemy out of a friend. You tell me that you will diligently inquire who it was that instigated the Prince to be so cruel toward you, and that once you know the truth you will take personal revenge against them. I must tell you that I am most saddened to read such words, as I am convinced that the virtuous man should never seek vengeance, no matter how great a pain is inflicted upon him. Therefore, in order to root out this unreasonable intention, you should keep in mind what has been said in the words of the Psalmist, that the man moved to bloodshed will not see the end of his days. This means that those who use the sword to cut short other people's days will surely see their own days cut short. The Psalmist goes on to say: "The man who is moved to bloodshed is evil and abominable in the eyes of God." This is illustrated by David when he says: "If you kill the sinners of God, the blood of men will be upon my head."[8]

If you think seriously about these matters I am sure that you will desist from your iniquitous and damnable purpose, and while making yourself amenable to useful advice, you shall leave vengeance to God, who justly metes out all retribution. I pray that He will grant you the beautiful virtue of patience.

FIFTH PERSONAL LETTER

Lady Helisenne to a lady named Galazia, whom she loves very much. Galazia has previously written that she is having an illicit love affair. Detesting this madness, Helisenne tries to persuade her to renounce it.

As I READ your letter, I took pity on you, for I realized that your misery is just beginning and there are clear signs that your reason is giving out. I am telling you this because it is clear that your soul is completely in the grip of vehement passion; your love is not grounded in virtue, and persisting in it will bring much reprobation upon you. How saddened I am at the thought of your future calamities! How true it is that love, as we often read, is a dream full of error, folly, temerity, and selfishness. It leads its followers to such extreme misery that their pain ends up seeming almost intolerable. Unquestionably, whoever is intoxicated by this venomous evil is deprived of rest. That is why Daedalus, a great architect of former days, cleverly made a hollow statue of Venus, which was always in movement because of the quicksilver he had placed inside.[9] One might interpret this as meaning that those whom love deprives of the great benefit of freedom never enjoy peace of mind.

The lesson is clear: in order not to succumb to this bondage, one must make an effort to resist it from the very beginning with a good and virtuous heart. From what you say whoever resists from the start can easily remain victorious. I realize that it hasn't been long since you were overtaken by this vain matter, and it may still be in your power to free yourself from it. You say that several considerations lead you to persevere in this love, for you believe that the man who holds your heart in thrall is endowed with so many qualities that in your opinion he is worthy of being loved by a goddess. You say that he is exceedingly handsome and as far as you can gather, you believe that true obedience, true love, and sovereign loyalty are to be found in him. In short, it seems to you that if future lovers should want to worship the world's most faithful lover, your friend would be the man to whom all would be obliged.

These illusions of yours prove your unawareness of the male character, which is to be very sweet at first, then very bitter. We commonly observe that after they have won a victory over their ladies, they aspire to new conquests, abandoning those whom they claimed to love forever. Pore through the history books; you will find that trust is betrayed and then remains broken. After these faithless, disloyal, lecherous men obtain what they want, they consider themselves lucky if they can habitually betray and get away with it. Not appreciating the advantages they received from women, this band of traitors repays feminine ingenuousness with their native ingratitude. Who was ever more humble and gracious in obtaining favor than Theseus? But once he had satisfied his lust with Ariadne he abandoned her all alone in a solitary place, as a wolf's quarry, a bear's prey, a lion's meat. Why? In order to ravish Phaedra, her sister.[10] Who ever showed a woman greater proof of friendship than the Trojan shepherd did to

Oenone? Yet he did not hesitate to repudiate her, after a perverse fortune allowed him to abduct Helen.[11] Who ever seemed more gentle than Demophon to his most gracious hostess Phyllis? And yet when he took his leave of her, he did not keep the sworn promise of a swift return. In so doing, he was the cause of Phyllis' death; for she was turned into a tree and began to flower when she sensed the arrival of her lover.[12] Who ever made greater use of deception than Jason toward Hypsipyle, whom he left, amid cries and tearful sighs and groans, as a reward for all the good she had done him?[13]

To tell the tale of all the ladies whom men have disdained would take more time than the restoration of Rome to the height of its ancient empire. Surely if you ponder these things, you will not have much trust in this fraudulent and deceitful masculine sex. I beseech you, begin to realize that a woman who trusts in them strips herself of freedom. Think and reflect that those who correct themselves from the example of others are most fortunate. Arm yourself, therefore, against the violence of love, and in calling reason back to the charge, wage war with yourself, persuading yourself that no one deserves as much praise for victory as one who fervently desires something and knows how to overcome one's appetites. Act in such a way that your virtuous and generous discretion brings you the same joy; and if you think that it is not within your power to root out this passion, you are wrong. One achieves as much as one sets out to do. Our soul is but a malleable form: we can mold it like a wax figure, adding or subtracting at will. Rejoicing comes as easily to it as sadness. Our life is what we make of it, nothing more, and where the will leads the soul will follow. Do as I tell you, then, and soon you will find that you won't suffer from following the straight path of reason. You will then be grateful for my advice and you will find that my lecture has served a useful purpose.

With this hope I shall end my letter, calling upon the Almighty that He may enlighten you with His grace.

SIXTH PERSONAL LETTER

Lady Helisenne to Meliadus, who is despondent because he has been stripped of some of his wealth. She consoles him with appropriate literary citations and reminds him that the wise man must not let transitory matters sadden him.

I'M SAD if you think I have been neglectful in sending you a letter of consolation. It was not my fault, as I was not aware of the misfortune that had occurred to you; my ignorance alone is to blame. I assure you that as soon as Rumor, which had spread in all directions, came my way, I readied my pen to show you that I am no less surprised than sorry at the thought of your misfortune. What causes me such astonishment is that you manifestly show that your strength of character no longer inhabits what I thought to be its permanent home.

When the rumor was confirmed that you showed signs of intense despair for having lost a great part of your wealth, I could not convince myself that this was so; I refused to believe it, but the rumor continued to spread. So then, telling myself that what so many people say cannot be entirely false, I began to believe in your well-known inability to bear up with misfortune. What appears to be sure from the detailed account I have heard is that your sorrow is so intense, you wail and weep so constantly, that had you drunk a quantity of water equal to your tears, it would pour superabundantly from your stomach and your grieving heart.

I don't know what misery makes you grieve and worry so over the vain and transitory things of this mortal world. We are here for a short time only, as the Psalmist demonstrates so aptly when he says: "Man's days are like straw and flowers, which quickly wilt and die."[14] You should also remember the contempt of wise people for temporal riches. Thinking them unimportant, the philosopher Socrates separated himself from them and threw them into the sea saying: "O deceptive wealth, I want to drown you, so that you will not drown me."[15]

In keeping with this same motif of contempt for the world, we read about Bias, one of the Seven Sages of Greece and resident of a city named Pryenne. Seeing that it was being besieged, he took flight. When the enemy interrogated him, and asked why he had not taken his many possessions, he answered: "But I have all my goods with me."[16] He said this because he did not consider his fortune to reside in transient things but in wisdom and strength of character. If Bias' reply is worthy of being remembered forever, so is that of Diogenes. When Alexander the Great asked him why he thought so little of him, Diogenes answered that he would have nothing to do with his servant's servant. Alexander was astounded to hear this and asked how he should interpret these words. Diogenes then gave him an immediate explantion: "I keep every lust and greed in check, including those that control you. But since greed is your master and you its servant, you are therefore in the service of what serves me."[17]

Surely those examples show that no treasure is enough to satisfy human appetite. But whoever lives reasonably finds that one can get by with little. Happiness and

fame are therefore bound to favor those who free themselves from an ambitious and insolent appetite. To this you
might respond that you don't feel contaminated with the
vice of avarice, that you were only hoping to preserve your
goods in order to take care of your needs, and that you did
not intend to accumulate a superfluous amount; but finding yourself in need is the reason why your heart feels such
an intolerable anxiety. Even if that were the reason for
your mental anguish, you should not despair. On the contrary, you must unfurl your sails with great courage, and
attempt to navigate in the waters of virtue with the oars of
wise discretion. If you are afraid of shipwreck you should
remember that the Creator of all things does not allow us
to perish through destitution. This is what He means in the
Gospel when He says: "Behold the birds of the sky, who
do not work, and yet your heavenly Father feeds them."[18]

If you do not keep these divine words in mind, then
you are less mature in mind than in years. You know that
you have already passed through several of the ages of man
as devised by Servius the Grammarian and by Varro.[19]
Have you not already left childhood, adolescence, and
youth behind? Now you are in the age which the divine
Plato describes: he says that when the eyes of the body begin to weaken and grow dim, the eyes of the soul begin to
fill with radiant light.[20] The diminution of bodily sight,
then, is accompanied by an increase of intellectual vision.
Therefore I beseech you, act your age!

How praiseworthy is he who shows consistency in the
face of adversity or persecution! O how many virtues remain concealed in many remarkable people for lack of being tested! And how many vices are hidden, for lack of the
means to commit them. Sometimes it is the strength of God
in us that prevents us from committing them. God's goodness is so great that it is always favorably disposed toward
us if we are disposed to receive it. Therefore I urge you as a

friend to turn toward God, begging Him to help you in
these pressing matters and to give you patience. Pray constantly, therefore.

Though the eternal God is ever disposed to be generous, yet He wishes to be implored, and for this reason
urges us to pray to Him, as is found in Saint Matthew:
"Ask, and it will be given you; seek, and you will find."[21]
These words of the Gospel show that frequent and assiduous prayers are most pleasing to God. These considerations should help you elevate your soul to God with faith,
hope, and love. If you do this, an inestimable consolation
will come to you. Believing it will come, I shall now end
my letter, imploring Him who shed His precious blood on
the wood of salvation to favor you with a special grace.

SEVENTH PERSONAL LETTER

Helisenne to Guisnor, whom she faithfully encour-
ages not to grieve excessively over the premature
death of his wife. She pleads with him to maintain his
faith in the soul's immortality.

I KNOW of no better way of consoling you than to tell
you of the sadness I am suffering on your account.
Having some indication that our pains are being shared by
our friends is the greatest relief against fortune's adversi-
ties. I can assure you that as soon as I had learnt that your
dearest companion had prematurely deceased, I fell prey to
a great anxiety which proceeded less from sorrow over her
departure than from fear that you would react impatiently.

While she lived there was a great bond of friendship

between us and it has in no way diminished in me. But when I think how blissful it is to be freed from the relentless miseries of this world, I consider her very happy; and the thought of her happiness is a source of comfort to me. How blissful to be safe from the dangers of outrageous Fortune and her sharp arrow; Fortune, that monster with the deadly tooth who tears, poisons, and kills those whom she has most favored. Now the power to harm her has been taken from your wife's enemies; neither envy, nor ambition, nor lust, nor sloth, can beset her anymore. Now her soul is in great joy; it has fled the body's prison and left behind its frail mortal parts. O death, you are the end of our toil, and the entrance to a safe port! If we saw things as they are, what we think is life we would call death; and what we think is death we would call life.

This is why many well educated people who have lost their friends bear up with their grief rather than torture themselves. While his son lay gravely ill, David did nothing but weep and wail; but as soon as the boy died, David stopped his lamenting and showed himself in public. When he was asked the reason for such a sudden change, the wise king replied that while his son was ill he grieved to see him suffering pain, and was not without hope of seeing him recover. But to mourn him now that his soul had been released from its coporeal dwelling was not only useless but sinful. For he felt more certain of following his dead son, than having his son return.[22] In this he showed his confidence in the soul's immortality. Empedocles did the same when he threw himself into the live volcano.[23] It was the same certitude that impelled Curtius to throw himself into the pit so as to save his fellow citizens from danger.[24]

We have so many other examples both ancient and modern that it would be too long and tedious for me to relate them. I should like to convince you, as you are wise, to let yourself be consoled by the certitude that the woman you loved so faithfully is still alive. Even if you tell me that it is not within your power to stop mourning, I know for sure that once you return to reason, your grief will be lessened. Think over what I have just written, remember your lady's most edifying life, and you will be persuaded that she is worthy of the company of God whose most holy teaching you know, and who rejects tears and lamentation as useless.

Why must you offend her memory by weeping constantly and wailing over her blessed change of state? Take comfort, and do not be ungrateful for this true and inviolable love, which she showed you in this world and which will continue to grow. Its fruition in God makes that love even more perfect now than it was then, and so she will pray for you fervently as you continue your worldy pilgrimage.

Those who are beatified, assumed into the court of heaven, and partake of the divine presence are all members of the Redeemer's mystical body and are perfectly united to Him as their Head. And as in the human body the strong, healthy members come to the aid of the weak and sick ones, likewise our dearly departed through their intercessions help to keep us from perishing in the perilous seas of this world. Here's a thought that should cheer you up. You must put an end to your constant weeping and wailing so that God will have mercy on you and make you worthy of His glory. You should recall how fortunate it is that the admirable virtues of this lady are worthy to be kept in perpetual memory; for wisdom, discretion, and temperance did make their home in her.

That lady had more virtue and grace in her than the rest of her sex combined. How favorable was divine mercy in allowing her body to die, while preserving her most illustrious virtues. Granted that she was gifted with wit, virtue, modesty, constancy, and saintliness; no one is so holy as to be above contamination, taint, or evil influence in dealing with the world. You should therefore give everlasting thanks to God, who allowed her to leave this world worthy of fame and praise, thereby protecting her from denigration through human weakness. If you but think of these matters you will be freed from all the anxieties that now bother you. I beseech the Creator of all things to bestow His grace upon you.

EIGHTH PERSONAL LETTER

Lady Helisenne to a friend of hers named Clarissa, exhorting her to break off a long love affair which is preventing her from complying with her father's wishes.

MY FAITHFUL FRIEND, if it is true that future events can be judged by past ones, I can be certain beyond doubt of the infallible and fervent love you bear me. There has always existed between us a bond not only of friendship, but of sisterly affection; consequently you must believe that the reading of your most sincere letter would have been supremely pleasant for me, had it shown me that you were happy of heart and tranquil of mind.

But knowing that you are beset by a most vehement sadness impels me to come to your aid; and though the thought of your anxiety disturbs me somewhat I do not wish to let my faintheartedness prevent me from advising you as to your honor and your personal security.

You tell me that your affliction results from paternal force pressuring you to marry that foreign gentleman who took up residence in your city some time ago. While I was there, as you know, I saw him come to your home a few times, and I noticed that he earnestly hoped to be approved of by your father, in order to have what you are still very reluctant to give; not because of his faults or imperfections, for as far as I can judge he is upright and honest both in his habits and his personality. But what compels you to go completely against the wishes of your family is your old, deep-seated love for a man you have spoken to me about several times. You have told me that the warm, kind love he showed you encouraged you to reciprocate in kind. I praised and approved this reaction of yours, as it was my considered opinion that whoever loves well is worthy to be loved.

Nevertheless, for the present, I want to convince you that for the sake of discretion, you cool the ardour of your thoughts and turn away from this love. The present situation is unpleasant for those who, whether out of a natural sense of duty or of concern for your welfare, are solicitous and watchful about your honor and well-being. So I beg you: give up this passion of yours and make your will obedient to your father's; bear in mind that if you are poor in advice you will be rich in worries; this alone should impel you to do what I sincerely advise.

If the memory of former pleasures is still fresh and makes you resist my advice, do keep in mind that it often occurs that marriages following upon a long love affair meet with an unfortunate end. The continuous jealousies, the strains, the loss of time, and the relentless effort lovers must make to keep their former passion alive is a fate worse than death. I am reminding you of all these things in order to convince you more easily to quell your amorous flame. If you cannot immediately desist, it is most urgent and indeed necessary to feign indifference and thus avoid showing what you wish to keep secret. Since I believe there is nothing in the world more deceptive than feigning the opposite of what one wants, I beg you to pretend to deny what you most desire so as to avoid arousing indignation in those who have control over you.

I am firmly convinced that being inclined to follow virtue, you will easily bear up with all forms of adversity. How praiseworthy it is to be firm in the face of misfortune, as I hope you will be. I am sure you will not wish to be counted in the number of faint-hearted women but rather will endeavor to imitate one whose steadfast endurance was her reason for changing her former name. I mean Helisa, subsequently called Dido, which in the Phoenician language means "Virago," one who exercises manly tasks. She was someone who did not give in to adverse fortune; just when fortune was attempting to crush her completely by sending her faithful husband to a premature death, Dido gave ample proof of her courage. Just as one sees the splendor of the stars shine in the dark of the night, so Dido, having fallen prey to dark misfortune, showed the splendor of her soul by building the great city of Carthage, which since then has become so very famous.[25] Everyone agrees that she was truly worthy of praise, for her great strength in such an extreme situation increased her constancy.

If you ponder this, she had greater reason to grieve over the loss of her dearest husband than you to be upset over the loss of a friend. You should realize that it is a far more grievous loss to be deprived of something one has possessed for a long time than of something one was looking forward to enjoying in the future. If you think matters over you will realize that your deprivation is rather of the latter sort. Yet, feminine virtue has but seldom resisted; should it do so in your case, it will serve as an example not only for our contemporaries, but for posterity as well. I believe in fact that the virtues of our ancestors can be rediscovered in their descendants. I am convinced that you are capable of such strength of character.

I shall end this letter, begging you not to betray the high opinion that I have of your wisdom.

NINTH PERSONAL LETTER

Lady Helisenne to the aforementioned Clarissa, encouraging her to persist in feigning indifference so as to give no sign of the passion which she has been unable to avoid.

YOU MAY BE SURE that I am quite worried about you, for I can tell from your replies to my letters that you are unable to root out from your heart a love that has for some time been planted there. But I take some measure of comfort in your telling me that you have managed to give no outward sign of your passion. You tell me that your father is putting constant pressure on you to have you obey his wishes, and that your only recourse has been to tell him that you have placed your trust in that one Spouse who promises eternal bliss to those who follow Him. Accordingly, you said, you had firmly decided to remain a virgin for the rest of your days. Your father was quite saddened to hear this and tried to remonstrate with you and to dissuade you from this supposed vow which he believes you have made. I'm told he said, among other things, that your status as his daughter does not allow you to make any vow without his consent, and that if your promise had been made impulsively, he could easily obtain its annulment from the Holy See.

You answered that though you could not deny being subject to him, you could, nevertheless, take any measure that you deemed necessary for your salvation. This was such an effective answer (you say) that your father stopped insisting, and with this subtle ploy you managed to defer a marriage for which you have no inclination. I should think you are quite happy to be freed from such a bother. I didn't dare urge you to rejoice beforehand, as I knew that your intense preoccupation would not make you receptive to advice. I'm sure you realize that this breathing spell can now help you in your own affairs. You have time to devise ways that will allow the man you love to tell your father of his deep affection for you. It may be that Fortune is tired of persecuting you and will favor you instead; if it does favor you beyond present expectation, be careful not to give an intemperate display of your love, which you have until now kept hidden with good sense, patience, and discretion.

I have wanted to warn you about this matter, not because I am unaware of the subtley of your mind, but so that my advice might give you further strength and bolster your constancy.

With this I shall close, asking God to give you happiness and peace.

TENTH PERSONAL LETTER

Lady Helisenne's second letter to her faithful friend Galazia, written with great apprehension, as she remembers how formerly she had reprimanded her about sexual passion. Now Helisenne confesses she has fallen in love.[26]

I FIRST took up my pen with the purpose of completely revealing to you some of my secret thoughts; but a number of considerations inclined me to retract this intention. Not that I thought you incapable of keeping a secret, for I am certain that you are anything but a flighty adolescent and that one should never hesitate in confiding in you. No, what really prevented and delayed my writing you was that I remembered having admonished you some time ago to avoid the discomfiture into which I myself have fallen; and so I thought you might in turn think me worthy of being reprimanded. I was so saddened by these thoughts of mine that, stripped of all hope of finding comfort, I was of a mind to hide my bitter, intolerable pain; but bearing in mind that hidden anxieties can only grow worse it has occurred to me that sharing them might bring me some relief. I have thrown my fear to the four winds; temerity has now taken it place, and has impelled me to begin the present missive, not, of course, without a preliminary flood of tears; yet my trembling hand will endeavor to bring solace to a heavy heart.

Alas! I don't know what name to give the pain I am suffering. If I say that my afflicted heart has been pierced by Cupid's arrow, it will answer that I made little effort to resist the assaults of this sublime deity. This objection is worth remembering, for if the heart were as pierced as we say, we should all die immediately. Where then, does this harsh passion reside? The rest of my body feels no pain; wherefore it must surely be located in my mind. Prey to troubling fantasies, my mind is filling my heart with an affliction for which there is no cure. But why should I be telling you these things? Have you not experienced them yourself?

I should rather try to explain to you what it is that troubles me and obstructs the satisfaction of my fervid and burning desires. I must give some thought to what I am about to say, lest I be accused of complaining for no reason at all. Indeed, when I think the matter over I realize I must not complain about love nor about the man I love: for I have fallen in love with a person so accomplished and handsome that none can match him. In addition, he is modest, graceful, well-spoken, and gentle, thus giving every indication of constancy and devotion.

What, then might you ask, can possibly obstruct my desires? Hoping for your consolation, I am telling you with tears and lamentations that adverse Fortune, flying through the air, has alighted upon me; and like a perverse sorceress she has added to my many woes by stirring up in me a hateful jealousy, which has conjured up the image of an ugly, wicked old woman, shaking continuously like a leaf on a tree. The name of this accursed old hag is . . . Fear. As you might well imagine she molested me beyond belief; but to repell her there appeared before me an old man with a happy, jovial face, uttering pleasant, loving words: his name is . . . Hope. He is always telling me to take courage, and his persistence has brought me some measure of consolation. I keep telling him: O Hope, refuge and consoler of those who fear, do not abandon me! Without you I cannot bear up with the anxieties which arise every day, with the pain which is my life's daily portion.

My dear friend, you can well imagine that even if I had no greater torment than my inability to speak to the man whom I am suffering for, my pain should still not be taken lightly. I assure you, in spite of my complaints, I should be beyond consolation were it not for the hope I derive from remembering that you, at least, got what you desired. This thought makes my love more intense, for as hope increases, so does desire. I am sure that reading my past writings will move you more to amazement than to pity; and remembering my earlier attitude you will say: "This woman, who thought she would not merely conquer love but rout it, has now been conquered in turn."

Though I imagine you shall utter these words, I shall at least ask you not to be surprised. Think how fresh green wood first rejects the fire's heat; but once aflame, it burns much longer and gives off a more intense heat. I too have been besieged, tempted and excited by love; persistent campaigns left me undefeated in the past; but one day I was overtaken by it, and today there is no woman more fervently and faithfully in love than I am. Now I shall cling to what I have dared admit openly. No task will wear me down, no peril will put me off; no accident will retain me nor prison hold me.

With this unswerving trust I shall end my complaint, imploring the Lord of heaven's host to give you a happy and prosperous life.

ELEVENTH PERSONAL LETTER

Lady Helisenne to the aforementioned Galazia. She is more afraid than ever to write her, as Fortune has been unfavorable to her love. She fears that the depressed tone of her letter will merely serve to dampen her friend's spirit.

I F FEAR once made me put off writing you, I have even less reason now to take up my pen; I am afraid that the dreadful news I am about to tell you will only make you sad. I am well aware that if telling pleasant news gladdens the soul, telling sad news afflicts and destroys the spirit. I had thought of giving you a belated account of my superabundant troubles. I was reluctant to do so, but that gentleman whom I have been unable to resist from the very first gave me explicit orders to inform you of my woes, withholding nothing.

With this encouragement, then, I must tell you: since my last letter I have been so viciously slandered that, unable to bear up under such an attack, I have fallen quite ill; for a while I longed for nothing else but to go off to that dark kingdom whose gate is kept by the triple-headed dog. But that small part within us which is the last to die kept putting off the dark powers of depression, unwilling to permit that the goddesses of the underworld perform an untimely exercise of their office.[27] But while my depleted body suffered such insidious woe, do you think my soul was free of anxiety? On the contrary: in my depleted condition hope preoccupied my mind in a way that words cannot tell; for the weak condition to which I had been reduced did not prevent me from remembering my beloved's beauty and youthful grace. I feared that my prolonged absence would give him an excuse to stop loving me and I kept telling myself it was to be expected that my beloved's affections should cool, being unrewarded for his service. Soon, I thought, he would cease remembering me.

All this made me very sad. Meditating on the fickleness of the human condition I thought it a cruel thing that a woman who had loved with such intense devotion should never obtain the reward she deserved. I thought surely I would be frustrated of what I wanted most. My mind was so continuously beset with these thoughts that they prevented my recovery.

My tribulation lasted for a long time, but at last Fortune allowed me to recover. But far from having satiated her jealousy toward me, she prepared for me a second blow more cruel than death: within a short time I learned that my lover had left the city. Apollo himself must not have felt more helpless when they told him that the child Hyacinthus was dying.[28] I was bitterly shaken, yet I had to hide my feelings; besides I was afraid that if I displayed my jealousy I should fall sick again. My pain was so great that

I might easily have died, had the dark of night not looked favorably upon at least one of my wishes, which was to be left alone. When I was at last rid of all my company I could open the floodgates of my tears which I had held back all day out of fear. In my depressed and lamentable state I would fantasize all sorts of things. I would remember the devices which society had thought up to destroy our love: I thought of the slanderers with their wicked tongues, who had so often managed to put such discord between us, only to have our love emerge more fervent and more full.

Experience has taught me that love can be compared to a fire: it dies quickly unless it is properly ventilated; on the other hand, continual stirring and prodding make it grow. So it is with lovers: an occasional irritation stirs and invogorates their love, which might risk dying out without an occasional stirring and ventilation. After spending some time thinking this matter over I would set it aside to inquire whether my lover could ever cease loving me. After giving *that* matter some thought I concluded that it could easily happen, seeing as how trouble and depleted energies are the greatest enemies of young love. I could not help reflecting, therefore, that if my lover persisted in travelling—which usually entails some measure of discomfort—he might well decide to cease loving me.

I was sorely afflicted by such thoughts; but was yet more stricken when I reflected that, should travel not deprive me of my lover, I might perhaps lose him by some other means. I cannot judge whether men are by nature quick to put you out of mind when they have put you out of sight. Convention supposedly has us assume that fickleness and mutability are the natural attributes of men. In any case, thinking about it did not raise any of my hopes, which had been making a noble attempt to cheer me up. Since hope has now left me I can assure you that I have been piling one depressing thought upon another; but to express them would be a relentless bore. Consequently I don't wish to add anything to the present letter, except to beg you for some consideration in this my darkest hour. I ask you simply to show compassion for my sorrow, as I have always done for yours.

I shall end this painful letter asking the Virgin Mother of God, who creates and sustains us, to preserve you from harm.

TWELFTH PERSONAL LETTER

Lady Helisenne to Quezinstra,[29] praising his faithful and benevolent friendship, which he had proved by using his eloquence to restore her to freedom.

M Y DEAREST FRIEND, I know that you have been hoping for some news about my present state; I must tell you that since the start of my captivity until now, I have been unable to temper my heart's anxieties. My pain, like the circumstances that gave rise to it, is so overwhelming that no words of comfort have succeeded in cheering me up.

But now that I have learned how by your eloquence you have endeavored to root out the vain and slanderous judgments which gave rise to my sorrow, I have cast off a part of my heart's despondency, as I think Fortune is not entirely hostile to me. Your tender affection for me does soften the pang of my stabbing pain. Now I know with certainty that nothing is comparable to the joy that a great friendship provides. That is why Alexander the Great's reply to his servants, which is cited as an oracle and was even usurped by Emperor Julian, is so justly famous. When they asked Alexander in a moment of great curiosity where he had placed his treasures and all his wealth he said: "I left them with my friends."[30] This answer shows us that a good friendship is to be preferred to worldly riches, which turn out to do more harm than good unless they are handled with discretion. Friendship is indeed a great gift; like good will and brotherly love it is a point of confluence of all things human and divine. For God has given to Man no gift more useful than wisdom, to which some prefer abundance of goods, others power, others honor, and many pleasure. Surely the latter preference is a sign of bestiality; as to the former they are fleeting, fragile and unsure, less obedient to our own dispositions and wishes than vulnerable to the whims of Fortune. And when Fortune decides to take something away from us, who is quicker to come to our rescue than a faithful friend? To a friend one can speak as if to oneself. How difficult it would be to tolerate adversity if we did not have a friend to share our affliction! But the enjoyment of prosperity itself would not be as pleasant if we did not have someone to rejoice with us.

Friendship, then, has the power to give greater lustre to prosperity and less weight to adversity. Whoever can count on the mutual affection of a perfect friend is indeed to be envied. Having experienced that sort of friendship with you I am sure of what I say. If I were asked whether your faithfulness has been tested, not wishing to hide your great qualities, I would answer: yes, a man's fidelity can be proved in three ways. First, if a new friendship does not diminish the friendship he had for me; second, if his prosperity does not so exalt him as to make him forget me; third, if my adversity does not make him leave me.

Friendship of this kind—true, stable, lasting, unchanging—is rarely to be found. For as Solomon says in the ninth chapter of Proverbs [sic]: "When shall the faithful man be found!"[31] As if he meant to say: it isn't easy. But if we are to believe our past experience, you surely deserve to be called a faithful friend, and I shall use every occasion to praise your virtuous constancy. If my praise falls far short of what you truly deserve, I beg you to blame it on the weakness of my style, and not to imagine that the insufficiency of my pen proceeds from ingratitude or negligence.

I don't know what else to tell you, except to beg you urgently not to discontinue remonstrating with my husband. Your eloquent words may finally make him understand how wrong he is to persecute and punish me. I hope you will succeed in persuading him, and I await your reply eagerly and with serene hope.

In closing, I pray the One who justly rewards all our deeds to bestow eternal happiness upon you.

THIRTEENTH PERSONAL LETTER

Helisenne writes at the urgent prodding of a gentleman who wishes to give one of his faithful companions some news about her. But since the information intended for the friend is of the most confidential sort, he requests that Helisenne write it cryptically, so that it will be unintelligible to anyone except the companion.[32]

I'VE SPENT SOME TIME looking at your letters, and I'm sure you think I intend to assail you and accuse you of being petty. I must tell you that such a thought has never crossed my mind. On the contrary: I think you are a virtuous and magnanimous person. The reason you think this way, is that you are under the impression that I am blinded by passion; you should know that I am even more eager to surrender the castle that you are besieging than you are to conquer it!

I'm sure your honest opinion of me will make you think that I am motivated by a foolhardy temerity or by an immoderate lust, rather than by the heartfelt and faithful love which I earnestly feel for you. This makes me sadder than words can say: for though you don't say it in so many words, you might tacitly inveigh against me and mentally accuse me of being inconsiderate. I do keep in mind, however, that in trying to resolve arduous problems, one must reflect before jumping to hasty conclusions. You might also tell me that if the debated question is a very periolous one, abstaining from combat may be a greater sign of strength than engaging in it, should the occasion be so warranted.

I have said all these things so as to assure you of my high regard for your clever mind which I am sure is better equipped than my poor wits not only to foresee what apparent disadvantages the future holds, but to preserve me from them as well. All things considered, if my wishes came true I should be in even greater peril than you. For if the vigilant and solicitous guardian of the castle (as you know, he has more eyes than Argus himself)[33] could have me in his custody after the commission of such an act, you can be sure that he would end my poor life with a miserable death; or at least that I should be more abandoned than the daughter of Nisus ever was.[34]

I never feared this before I met you. But the day I first came into your enfolding presence I wanted so much to give you my favor, that the fear of death itself left me. You heard me tell you this myself, and you should not doubt my words, for they have been borne out by my actions. Think how great is the love I bear for you in my heart. Surely if one is to trust experience you should have some inkling of my love. So if your mind is still preoccupied with the same thoughts as earlier, I beg you, stop. For I swear to you that nothing—except heartfelt love—impelled me to commit that unjust act; but if I loved you with a fervent love before, what must I do now? Unless I wish to be guilty of the basest ingratitude it will grow even more, since your pertinent counsel was so helpful to me in such important matters.

I am pleased to have been able to show that if one's desire is occasionally stirred up, it can also be tempered with reason, arrested with good counsel, corrected with discretion, and restrained with moderation. You are young in years but old in wits: in your youth you are blessed with a maturity that many lack in their old age. I find this trait in you so praiseworthy that, knowing the incapacity of my frail spirit, I would rather pass over the rest of your qualities in silence than continue in this vein, since your wisdom deserves a better eulogist than me. Since, however, you are a model of urbanity and forbearance I trust you will imitate the king of Persia, who was more sensitive to sincere feeling than to common expression. Trusting in that sincerity I can recover enough composure in order to respond to the overtures you claim to be about to make, thereby satisfying my loving desire, and giving evidence of your own willingness to gratify me.

You tell me you are ready to give wings to your obedience in order to accomplish whatever would be pleasing and acceptable to me, even at the risk of falling into the same peril as Icarus. I can assure you that remembering the discretion with which you spoke to me on another occasion I am astonished; but knowing how invincible is the power of love, I believe you. However, if truth be told, before reaching your present resolution, you witnessed in yourself a great debate between your extreme prudence and your excessive love. I ask you: if your love was that strong how could you possibly act differently from anyone else in love? It is of course not a new thing that men of science are sometimes forced through the instigation of people they love to give in to illicit things. Daedalus, the maker of the Cretan labyrinth, was unable to resist the importunity of his son Icarus. He therefore allowed the young adolescent to use the artificial ingeniousness which he himself had invented in order to avoid the ill treatments of Minos.[35] I also remember the splendid Apollo who, persuaded by Phaeton's presumptuous request, allowed him to lead the swift horses Pirous, Eous, Ethon, and Phlegon. But his allowing this led to serious consequences, for that is how the Ethiopians acquired their black color.[36]

But in your opinion it is those who do the asking who are to be blamed, isn't it? As far as I can judge, it should not be blamed on someone else. Whoever gets into trouble through his own fault should not blame another. But it would be just the opposite with you, since to show how flexible you are in obedience to me you would be ready to put both of us in great peril. I blame myself, not wishing to deny that it is I who am to blame, and if it ever came to pass that because of my audacity (which I know to exceed that of all people past, present, and future) I were to lose you (whom I love more than the great-souled son of Thetis ever loved his dearest companion Patroclus),[37] what life would then be mine, assuming I should survive?

I assure you that I can foresee two consequences, the lesser of which would be enough to drive me out of my mind. The first would be that my iniquity would be immediately divulged: for the goddess Rumor (who, according to the Ancients, was born of Vesta after the death of the Giants) would take to flight with her agile feet and her great, light wings,[38] not allowing such things to be hidden. And secondly, there would be as many people despising my miserable life as there would be mourners of your unfortunate death. Surely I cannot distinguish which of the two one should feel sadder about: perverse people who live, or virtuous people who die. For the evil which remains causes no less anxiety than the good which perishes. It is indeed a painful thing to see good people die: but surely it is no less painful to see evil people live. Yet conceivably I would not only be molested by Argus, but all honest people would delight in hurting me so as to help him. I would thus be the cause of scandal; my inability to resist such oppressions could lead me to that ultimate ill, death. The other cause leading me to extreme anxiety would be my awesome pain should I be deprived of you, a pain more violent than the one King Priam felt over the deplorable loss of his children and the devastation of his kingdom.[39]

I am not telling you these things as a warning, for I am sure they are already engraved in your brilliant mind. This has sufficed in order to give my own mind some light, although I was quite troubled at first by my separation from a woman whom I am unable to call back to my presence. But you may be sure that I am telling you these things in order to let you know that your kind words have taken. I can therefore assure you that if until now I persuaded you to take the castle in every way possible, I should now like to consent that you lift the siege for a while. But during that period I don't want you to cease meditating some of the least perilous and most appropriate ways of conquering it; yet I want you to feign the contrary impression, remembering Caesar who always tried to appear desirous of peace and rest, while carefully preparing military tactics. You know full well that there is nothing more disquieting for someone else than dissimulation.

Therefore I believe that since you see more clearly

than I do in these matters, you will rejoice over the advantages I have derived from your science; and I should be inclined joyfully to talk about it, but cannot. For I cannot accomplish what you persistently ask of me, which is that I receive a messenger sent by you, for just one hour, so that he might impart some secrets to me. Alas, my good friend, this request of yours proves that you have not been warned about the injuries and the contempt, in fact and in word, that were levelled against me. Argus, that hundred-eyed monster, suspected that I had talked to you; and to incriminate me he said that, together, we had devised a subtle plot to take his castle from him.

Nevertheless I always denied this with a straight face, so much so that my continual persistence prevailed. But as Fortune is not yet content to agitate, afflict, and persecute me, having seen me resist the dangers of the monster Scylla, she has plunged me into the depths of the maelstrom Charybdis.[40] I am telling you this, because there came to me an unhappy and wretched creature who, in keeping with ancient custom, is ceaselessly subverting our unanimous wills, and intends to persevere in doing so. For far more than you can believe she delights in committing and perpetrating iniquities, as she has been addicted to vice since her youth and they have become as second nature to her. Her heart is so intoxicated with venomous malice that it is certain that poison would be unable to kill her: for one poison can easily neutralize the other. I should very much wish that you had seen her in the heat and impetuosity of her anger, for I believe that had you done so you would take pity on me, seeing me subjected to this accursed person who is no less vigilant than Argus. I wish Mercury, the God of eloquence, would have put them to sleep with the sound of his pipe, allowing me to go to you.

But alas, since this thing I so desire cannot be, I see nothing that can presage future consolation to me, unless I am certain that you want to believe that my will is entirely submissive to yours. If I were free, it would be unnecessary for you to beg me so much; for I can assure you, my friend, that your wish would be my command, and you would find me quite ready to obey. Therefore I beg you: knowing my words are sincere, and in keeping with your usual kindness, pray hold me excused. I also beg you not to be angry with me if in the future I cease, in turn, having your faithful messenger bear news to you. Because of the continual presence of the aforementioned Monster, it would be beyond my power to send the messenger back to you; even if I were to receive him and find a quiet place to entrust him with my news, this would be a sure sign that I have secrets to tell. All secret speech invites suspicion, and that is what strips me of all hope. Therefore I can assure you that I shall be in persistent and continuous sorrow until the end of my tormented life.

I should like to write you many other things, were it not that the soul's passions, coupled with the body's infirmities, force me to end this epistle. May the Sovereign of Heaven preserve you in happiness and prosperity forever.

Here end the Personal Letters of Lady Helisenne.

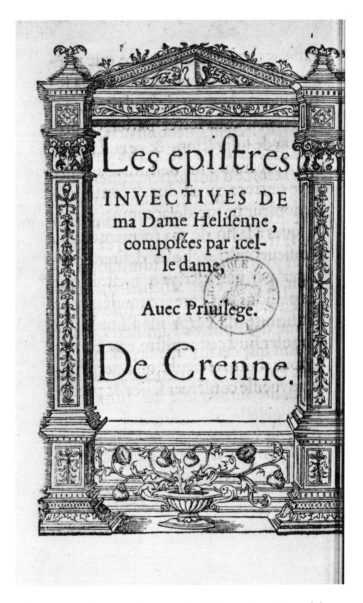

Les epiſtres

INVECTIVES DE
ma Dame Heliſenne,
compoſées par icel-
le dame,

Auec Priuilege.

De Crenne.

Title page to the second section, *Les Epistres Invectives*, of the
1539 edition of Helisenne's letters, published by Denys Janot.

The INVECTIVE LETTERS of
LADY HELISENNE de CRENNE

PREAMBLE

O EAR READERS, you are all aware, as am I, of the difficulty of keeping one's patience so constant and so strong as to not let oneself be overcome by excessive agitation. You should not be surprised, then, if in my present state of constant anxiety I forego the usual style of the Personal Letters, as I realize that the adversity of Fortune does not allow me to persevere in that vein. Her insufferable cruelty so pricks my anger that rather than follow my natural inclination, I feel compelled to write Invective Letters instead.

How many opportunities does Fortune, with her criminal ways, allow us to loathe her and inveigh against her! As I lament my fate inconsolably and with good cause I tell her: "O wicked Fortune, you who have become Goddess of this indifferent world, how is it that your wheel is always turning for the benefit of others? Don't you see, cruel woman, how loathsome a thing it is to remember your ways? Consider how burdensome is this variability and inconsiderateness of yours. You favor and praise to the skies those who despise you, yet you visit calamity and misery upon those who, with honor and supreme reverence, sacrifice to you. For this reason you may be quite sure that your inveterate ingratitude makes you a fitting target for the hatred of others."

I call to witness those who have known your deadly persecutions first hand. Given the diversity of your effects, I ask them what sort of face one should show you. If their opinions concur with mine there is perhaps no better way of representing you than the following: we read that in the old days, on the banks of the Tiber in Rome, a temple was raised to Fortune. According to Saint Augustine (*City of God*, III, 18 [*sic*]) Fortune was seated in the center of a wheel which she spun continuously.[41] She had two faces, one beautiful and resplendent, the other very difficult to see, indicating that those whom she loves and looks at with the right face are happy, while those whom she harms are miserable and unhappy. Thus depicted as blind, she was shown as having no respect for people's merit but rather sustaining the good and the bad indiscriminately. Now you can understand why Fortune's face is so insidious. She spins the human race around in a manner quite in keeping with her symbol; and were it not for divine Providence, which often robs her of her perverse strength, it would be impossible to disarm her of her furor.

Filled as I am with concern for you, dear friends and readers, I am giving this matter my serious consideration; and I implore divine mercy that, while preserving you from Fortune's iniquity, she bestow on all of you a happy and prosperous life no less durable than that of Nestor, the master of eloquence.

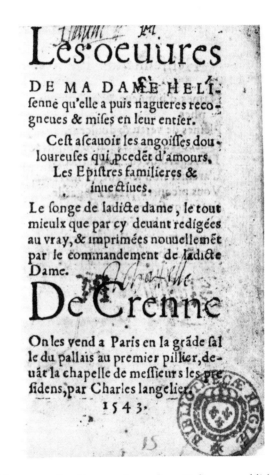

Les·oeuures

DE MA DAME HELI-
senne qu'elle a puis n'agueres recogneues & mises en leur entier.

Cest ascauoir les angoisses douloureuses qui pcedēt d'amours,
Les Epistres familieres &
inuectiues.

Le songe de ladicte dame, le tout
mieulx que par cy deuant redigées
au vray, & imprimées nouuellemēt
par le commandement de ladicte
Dame.

De Crenne

On les vend a Paris en la grāde sal
le du pallais au premier pillier, de-
uāt la chapelle de messieurs les pre
sidens, par Charles langelier.
1543.

Title page to *Les Oeuvres de ma dame Helisenne*, published by
Charles Langelier in 1543.

FIRST INVECTIVE LETTER

Lady Helisenne to her husband. She wishes to persuade him that he is wrong to make himself her enemy and to make her suffer without cause. She chastises him and accuses him of cruelty.

I REALIZE that seeing my unsolicited letter will make you wonder at my temerity in writing you once again, knowing as I do of the unflagging hostility which you have nurtured against me for such a long time, a hostility so fierce that I fear it will keep you from even reading this letter. Yet if you were a man of mature judgment, you would restrain your impetuous anger. You have without cause made me suffer so many and such extreme misfortunes that, had I committed the most heinous of crimes, I could not be more punished. You have brought public reprobation upon me with all its attendant pains. Why? Because you lend a too willing ear to my detractors. This ignorant, servile lot has made you credulous, and believing them has put you in a state of mind from which you have been unable to free yourself.

Your heart's hasty judgment has led you to imagine that my *Angoysses* (which I had composed, in fact, only to pass the time) were intended to immortalize an illicit love. You believe, moreover, that I really experienced the lasciviousness about which I wrote. I am surprised you should imagine this to be the case, for as I was modest and temperate in my young and tender years you cannot allow yourself to believe that I am lascivious now that I am older. Tell me, what is it that always makes you consider things in their worst light? In doing so, you convey the impression of a man so disturbed as to be deprived of his true judgment. It is plain enough to see that had you looked at my writings calmly, you would have changed your mind. If your anger were grounded in reason rather than in your desire to persecute me, I should like you to consider the number of instances in my writings where I disapprove of illicit love. Haven't you noticed how often I plead with the women of this and any age to live decently? Any prudent and discreet man should know that my heart is chaste and pure; and in order to be so, it hopes that all others will preserve a similar integrity.

You should remember something I know to be true: when a licentious and whorish woman has put modesty behind her, what she desires most is to make other women fall into a similar whorishness. You should certainly realize that being a lascivious woman is the furthest thing from my mind. But alas! I am afraid you do not want to set your mind to any thoughts as reasonable as these so as to pursue your violent anger with me. I fear that you will persist in your unstinting opinion, compelling you to insult me as a matter of course.

One of the more outrageous statements you have made while insulting me is to tell me that my very words are the proof of my guilt. You accuse me of having admitted to you that I was violently overcome by sexual passion. I certainly remember being crushed by the excessive vigor with which you persecuted me. My patience was at end. I could no longer bear your torments. You unleashed your anger beyond the control of reason, so gaining the upper hand; because of my words you proclaimed me guilty of that which had never stained my innocence. O how loathsome is my fortune! For in my hour of grief you silenced your discretion and allowed your anger to speak. I can now understand why powers above and below were against me: for more than anything else, despair had taken its toll.

I say these things because every day we witness people committing some vicious act, and should their conscience accuse them, they try to relegate to the shadows the evil act they have committed. No rational person wants to admit his turpitude. Do consider the calamity I have been led to by my adverse fortune and by your cruelty, since they accuse me of having done something the very thought of which had never occurred to me. Alas, if you recall my way of acting at the time, you should remember that if I uttered some words that went beyond my thoughts it was only to pretend that death would put an end to my pain; for I expected that, as you were crueller than cruelty itself, you would swiftly put an end to my life.

But I cannot imagine, once you had heard my words, what prevented you from executing this last wish of mine. Perhaps it was through some grace of God, who, realizing the pretense of my wanting to die, did not allow me to do so; for the passion which had overcome me and the anger which had deprived me of my true feeling would have justified your having a bad opinion of me. I was hoping to eradicate that opinion with a chaste and modest life. I wish to warn you that the very person with whom you share your secrets has disclosed your present opinion of me. It has been made clear to me that you are doing everything in your power to obstruct the satisfaction of my desires, deeming beyond doubt that I have stained my chastity, if not in deed, then in desire. Surely your superfluous words make it clear that you have not yet had enough of contaminating my reputation. I am surprised that you do not realize that the infamy which you bring down upon an innocent person like me rebounds upon you. Tell me, do you really think that in diminishing my good name you will increase yours? Do you really imagine yourself to be the caring husband of a woman whose heart, according to you, is totally perverted? Should you presume this, it is clear that you are profoundly mistaken. Should you continue in your bitterness, your efforts will not succeed, and for the following reason: I am certain that those to whom you once praised my chastity will not believe to be true your account of my licentiousness. Do you really think them ready to believe that I am in the service of that little god Eros known to set hearts aflame with an unquenchable fire?

Seriously, no one will expect that your protesting against a passion as violent as love is enough to prevent love's desires from getting what they want. In a matter like this one I find that my opinion rather conforms to the generally accepted one. I shall, therefore, speak of love (not because I have learned this through experience, but because literature has taught me to understand) to demonstrate to you that so far as lovers are concerned no obstacle to their passion is ever too great. Do you not remember those two perfect lovers from Babylon who died next to the crystal fountain?[42] Do you not realize that in doing away with all inhibitions their passion led them to a miserable death? If the arrival of that cruel lion had not caused their death, what power could possibly have prevented them from enjoying everything that love can afford, for they considered themselves distinct from other people?

How I admire the audacity and daring that a defiant Cupid imparted to his servants! Paris and Helen are an outright demonstration of such daring, they who were the talk of all Asia and Europe. You do know, of course, that when the handsome young foreigner and the Greek lady first set eyes on each other their desire so bound them that they quickly consummated their deadly passion. Neither the fear of public slander nor the obvious price they would have to pay could prevent them from bringing the affair to its conclusion.

Were I to continue relating to you the infinite number

of lovers who exposed themselves to deadly peril, not only would the tale be tedious for you but it would be painful for me. Please make an effort, in any case, to root out your damnable opinion of me, for you can be sure that had I sunk into lasciviousness as you so claim, you would not have succeeded in keeping me from it. Had ingenuity kept me from gratifying my desire, you can be sure love and temerity combined would have encouraged me to investigate further. If your perverse fantasies could only give way to more fitting thoughts, you might be convinced that I have kept myself pure in thought and in deed, not through your solicitude, but through the purity of my own will. How happy I would be if my heart's integrity could be tested as was the virginity of Claudia, the Vestal Virgin! Though Claudia was accused of not having bridled her sexual desire, Fortune was not so harsh as to prevent her from proving her innocence. The goddess Vesta was most responsive to Claudia's need for vindication: as a statue of the goddess was being shipped from Phrygia to Rome (as told in Philometor, 28), the chaste Claudia tied a rope to the prow of the ship where the statue of the goddess was stored and prayed, "O Mother of the Gods, if I am chaste, give me the power to pull this ship." The goddess Vesta was unsparing in her help, for Claudia was easily able to pull the ship by herself with a small rope, a feat which a herd of horses could not have reproduced. In fact, Claudia dragged the ship over dry ground all the way back to Rome, and that was how she won her reputation back![43]

I also remember reading in the twenty-second book, eleventh chapter of the *City of God* about a virgin who was once accused of having committed fornication. To prove the accusation false and demonstrate her virginity, she miraculously carried water in a sieve.[44] When I remember such instances as these I cannot help invoking the name of many goddesses in order to find out if one of them will not come down to vindicate me. It seems unquestionable that if the goddess Vesta was diligent enough to intercede for the virgins entrusted to her care, the goddess Juno should not be remiss in bringing help to married women who have fervently obeyed her chaste laws.[45] Why she puts off coming to my assistance is a mystery to me; perhaps it's to allow me to prove my patience and my incredible tolerance! Once I have demonstrated that, I also hope to convince you that in so undermining my sense of honor you have committed a grievous offense. I shall end here, imploring God in His goodness to free you from your misguided opinions.

SECOND INVECTIVE LETTER

Lady Helisenne's husband's reply. He insults her repeatedly and concludes that all the anxiety she thinks she suffers is nothing compared to what she has caused. In loathing her he loathes the entire female sex.[46]

AFTER RECEIVING your mendacious letter I was not as surprised as you thought I would be, for the simple reason that I am not unaware of your presumptuous nerve. But I must confess I am astonished to see you so confident in your subtlety as to think you can lead me to believe that I became your enemy without cause. If I understand you correctly you seem to think that the clarity of my judgment is clouded; and imagining this to be the case you then go on to give a prolix account of the anxieties you supposedly suffered. I don't know whether you were as hurt and anxiety-ridden as you say you were, but I am sure that I could not possibly inflict upon you the punishment your iniquitous behavior deserves.

Your loathsome person has so offended me that, having only one life you could not possibly make sufficient amends by losing it. To be punished as you deserve, your wretched body would have to be raised up countless times. Indeed, the pain of many cruel and ignominious deaths might be sufficient amends to erase the hateful stain of your monstrous sins.

You inveigh against me, saying that I am too quick to lend credence to your detractors. That is why you tell me that my credulousness is what incited me to have a bad opinion of your writings; and to rid me of these fantasies you come to remind me of the sincerity of your past conduct. In this matter you hope to make me believe that you have never swayed from the path of virtue. Surely it wasn't necessary to tire your hand recording your past life in written form. I often think back to the reputation you had for being a repository of chastity. You were so resplendent with that virtue that I was ready to believe that in my absence your continence would have been comparable to Penelope's.[47] I didn't hesitate to consent to your travelling, thinking you equipped with the sails and rudders that allow good women to escape the maelstrom that engulfs lesser souls.

Whoever would have thought that you, gifted as you are with the graces, would ever have allowed yourself to drown in the depths of unbridled lust? Instead you robbed me of that hope, you divorced and repudiated Lady Virtue, and you stored within you the very opposite vices. These accumulated within you to destroy the rudders of your virtue: you raised the anchors of your shame, you unfurled the sails of your heart, and your ship dashed itself against the rocks of lust. Surely, unless you really want to pursue these artificial and colorful lies of yours, you will cease contradicting me. You know, of course, that once your desires were kindled you were unable to keep dissimulating them. Your heart, aflame with a lustful fire, ardently aspired to do so but could not; therefore I don't want you to think that it is your accusers or your writings which generated the bad opinion I have of you. I assure you that if I am credulous it is not about things heard but things seen.

As to the arguments you propose for your defense, such as your warning other ladies to be careful, you mustn't think that this trick will succeed in hiding your detestable vices. However much you may think that your writings bear out your invulnerability to lust, it is notorious that all women who are contaminated by that disease want to see other women similarly infected. That fleshpot Queen Semiramis[48] certainly bears this point out: she was so fired up with her need for sex that she instituted a law, which was enacted immediately, allowing her subjects to fornicate as much as they pleased. This conforms very much with your own thinking, and you must not try to protest your innocence. Everyone knows you are more subtle than other women and persuade them to be chaste while pretending to be good yourself. You must not think that the soul's secrets are invisible or that I am unaware of your perverse intention, which you conceal only because you are afraid of being cast out of the company of women. In your writings you have not as yet divulged the perversity of your will; but these virtuous protests of yours, of which you are so proud, will be of little use to you; for sometimes an honest intention yields a sinister and perverse result. I am telling you this because I know your ingenuity will ultimately serve no other purpose than to encourage other women secretly to commit what you pretend to loathe.

You tell me that you fear I shall continue to flail you with persistent insults and reproach you for having said that you were passionately in love with someone. Not wishing to deny this, you then excuse yourself by saying that your ill fortune, coupled with my ill treatment of you, was the main reason for your saying you would rather die than live, and thus free yourself from my cruelty. I beg you: don't accuse fortune or me. I deny that I am cruel: for justice and cruelty are different things. I assure you that even if you had not said a word I had enough evidence against you. Believe me, a guilty conscience accuses itself. The eye cannot conceal the fault that is engendered in the heart: your dreary face has been your own worst enemy.

You yourself admitted that you were unhappy. You admit you were surprised that I did not kill you after listening to you. Then, speaking to your best advantage, you state things that are far removed from the truth when you pretend it was divine mercy that dissuaded you from putting an end to your days. I don't know what could have moved you to say these things, since you know that nothing is concealed from God's foreknowledge: I'm sure He sees the malice in your heart. Not wanting the sinner's damnation but rather his conversion, God in His goodness has kept you alive for a while in order that some holy person might beg and pray divine mercy to send you His grace; being truly contrite and repentant you might submit to corporal punishment in order to avoid the eternal punishment of the soul.

As I've pursued the reading of your letter nothing has surprised me more than your accusing me of having told so many lies about you. You say for example that I pride myself in being so subtle that in spite of your lustful nature I have restrained myself from punishing you physically. To these lies of yours let me answer, wretched woman, that not content with tormenting me, you want to make me the bearer of your guilt and blame; so much so that I believe that you wish to take out the crimes you have committed on my poor innocent self.

It is high time you silenced your libidinous tongue. I

needn't listen to one of your endless narratives in order to understand that people in love are apt to think up any old trick in order to indulge in the venereal act. I know what I'm saying: everybody knows that when women are prevented from satisfying their lascivious desires they become remarkably daring. Take the case of Scylla: she was passionately in love with Minos. In order to endear herself to him and draw his affection she furtively deprived her father of the crucial strand of hair which was his only means of preserving his kingdom.

Several other examples come to mind, but since I don't wish to bother detailing them I simply want to tell you that your attempts to persuade me are to no avail. You tell me, for example, that since I admit your words do not have a corrupting effect you must then be sincere in your thinking. I must tell you that I in fact mistrust both your thoughts and your actions; and I cannot imagine how your lying tongue could go so far as to say that you would be most happy if your chastity could be tested as was the virginity of Claudia and of another virgin (whose name you have omitted). How I would love to see you pray to Juno's statue and in proof of your chastity attempt to draw her ship after you, as Claudia did that of Vesta! Except that you wouldn't have the same luck as Claudia. For this goddess Juno, Jupiter's sister and paramour, would want the news of your adultery publicly diffused. Not only would she show her just anger toward you by depriving you of the strength to pull the ship; believe me, as further proof of your iniquity she would pull you right into the waves to drown you in the dread darkness of the dreary deep. If perchance to prove your innocence you did not elect to draw the ship, neither should you attempt to put water into a ship so full of holes; for not only would the liquid evaporate, but to further confirm the reality of your abominable lust the ship would be so dashed to pieces that the splinters would pierce you and send you reeling off to Hades! Your soul would quickly be sacrificed to the gods of the under-world who, knowing it to be polluted and infamous, would send it off to its eternal punishment with the accursed shades.

Do give some thought to the danger that your abominable sins put you in: so great they are in number that I shudder to recall them. What miserable creatures you are, you and those like you—and there are so many of your kind! For the seed of fidelity has been sown so little in this fickle female sex. O fraudulent womankind! The more we believe you the more we are deceived; the more we lend you the more we lose; the more we love you the more we are offended.

That is why we must count happy those who shun you deceiving creatures. There have been many warnings against marriage in literature; but those who have written these things have not demonstrated as much pain, toil, and trouble in all their writings as has any one woman provided her husband in a single day. O how the wise man should think twice before submitting himself to a woman in the connubial bond! For he must open his heart wide and accept all that customarily comes with her. Remember Socrates who patiently tolerated so much grief from Xanthippe that he considered all women malicious. Once, being asked what he thought of women, he said they reminded him of a tree called Adelfa—beautiful to look at, but full of poison. Somebody asked him why he encouraged people to shun women. He answered: because I see women habitually avoiding good and seeking evil.[49]

How right he was! Surely there is no more proud or perilous enemy of man than woman. O poor dumb shades of men now departed, who before your death were tormented by them, how I wish you could now come back to life to testify to the truth of what I say! What would Hannibal say about Tamira if he could come back to life? What would Mark Antony say of Cleopatra? Philip of

Macedonia of Olympia? What would Samson say of Delilah? What would Nero say of Agrippina? I dare think that anyone willing to listen to their complaints would find a convincing argument to avoid you all![50] How dangerous are your powdered allurements, the source of so much grief. The literature that mentions beautiful Greek, Latin, Egyptian, and Roman women does not remember them for their beauty but for the grief that their beauty caused. How I wish we could quarantine them! Alas! The spirit is willing but the flesh is weak. The war between reason and the senses is a great one; and that's what makes us fall right into their traps. Yet I keep warning the young and exhorting the old, arousing the wise and instructing the naive to pray and supplicate the Almighty for a sovereign remedy to avoid your ensnaring nets. To this same Power I pray that He might divulge that which I already know about you from experience.

THIRD INVECTIVE LETTER

> Helisenne to her husband. She accuses him of slander, the most damaging of vices because it incriminates all of womankind. Helisenne finds this intolerable and lists several arguments in refutation of her husband's opinion.

EVERY DAY your deadly hatred against me intensifies. I cannot hide the effect that your recent letter had on me. I must warn you that it helped me understand one thing: your condition is that of a madman who enjoys indulging in self-destruction while engaged in destroying someone else. You are so puffed up with your arrogance that when reason fails, you can only have recourse to slander, rage and insult. But I assure you that what you say is far less painful to me than what you force me to tell you. I should refrain from doing so had your malevolent words been addressed only to me; indeed you may be sure that my heart is so accustomed to suffering that it would have been easy for me to hide my pain. Besides, I know that insults hurt the attacker even more than the victim.

Seeing as how you loathe the whole feminine condition, however, it has seemed to me that your insult is particularly great because it is universal. I shall therefore be silent as to your accusations against me in particular and concentrate on refuting your incrimination of what you call our malevolent deeds. If my memory serves me right the first of your accusations is that women are unfaithful, inconsistent, fraudulent and deceptive—in short, if anyone were to believe what you say, no one would ever get married.

I don't know what makes you despise that institution so, as it has been instituted by God and has been esteemed so highly that Scripture has compared the state of the Church to the state of marriage, calling the Redeemer a bridegroom and the Church his bride. The state of marriage has been praised not only by Scripture but by the Natural Law and all of classical pagan literature. Everyone should endeavor to praise it as it deserves. What you say about Socrates, who suffered so greatly at the hands of his dreadful wife, does not amount to much. If you say that Socrates categorically railed against all women, you must remember that he himself belonged to the category of henpecked husbands. Therefore anything he saw bearing the same form, likeness or resemblance to that which caused him such annoyance, Socrates judged apt to produce a like evil.[51] Because one woman was the cause of that philosopher's annoyance, Socrates thought that any woman coming within his sight was as malevolent as Xanthippe. His annoyance prevented him from seeing things clearly.

Notwithstanding this you might wish to pursue your diatribe, adding that Solomon and the Book of Wisdom despised the female sex and warned against Woman's deception, Woman's iniquity, and the mellifluous accent of a foreign woman.[52] They have written many other things about bad women, but you must understand that this is a marvelous way of promoting good women. These, the aforenamed Solomon and the Book of Wisdom have praised, writing that in a woman of valor and strength the heart of a husband can find peace.[53] They also state that Woman is Man's crown, the adornment of his home, his consolation and his joy. These are words of truth. What rejoinder could you possibly give?

Surely it is pointless for you to say that feminine beauty with its sumptuous dress is both vain and dangerous. To lend substance to your argument you remind us yet once more of the perils into which men have fallen in the past for having been fascinated by women's beauty. But if one reflects on this matter, it is not women who should be blamed, for if men are supposed to be wiser than women they should not deal with anything they know to be harmful or dangerous. Though men consider themselves rational they forsake reason for sensuality; then they blame women for making them succumb.

For the sake of sheer honesty, it seems to me, they should not proffer such lies. They should be ashamed to say that they have been deceived by women. What a shameful injustice it is for men to fault women for deception when in their heart of hearts men know that they are always the ones doing the deceiving. From the moment a man casts a lustful eye on the genuine beauty of a woman's face he is in constant pursuit of her and tries to conquer her no less persistently than if he were besieging a city with war machines. So loathsome is the malevolence of lustful men that the more virtuous the women, the more vulnerable they are to men's ways. We read in literature that it was not the beauty or even the gentleness of Lucretia, that flower of modesty, which stirred up the mad audacity of an incestuous Tarquin to rape her, but rather the lady's wholesome, pure and sincere life.[54]

Nevertheless you spend your time blaming women for their physical beauty: I can assure you it holds no danger for any man of integrity. If womanly beauty were as destructive as you say it is, the children of Israel would not have been allowed to select beautiful women from among their prisoners and captives, as found in Deuteronomy.[55] We read of Abraham's servant that when he laid eyes on Rebecca he wondered whether this was the woman whom God had meant for Isaac.[56] I also remember the example of Abigail, the wife of Nabal, a most evil man. She was no less wise than beautiful, which allowed her to preserve her husband's life and possessions in spite of David's ferocity; and thus was that iniquitous husband saved by his wife's beauty. For David said to her: "Go up in peace to thine house; see, I have hearkened to thy voice and have accepted thy person.[57] If you ponder this, surely, you will admit that you are wrong to hold in contempt what is held up for others to admire.

As to what you have said about women's willingness to experiment in rich and sumptuous clothes, Jerome has written that women and girls desire expensive clothes; and he knew several chaste women who did so, not in order to satisfy foolish men nor out of pride, but out of honest regard for the social state of their husbands or fathers.[58] So affection too is a consideration. You might tell me that men are drawn into lasciviousness and lust by the way women dress, as the seventh book of Proverbs says.[59]

Women not bound by matrimony, who adorn themselves in order to please their lovers or any other man, offer an occasion to sin and incite to sin. If they do so they are guilty of serious sin; and if such is your opinion you are not far from the truth. But women who dress simply to satisfy a small need for glory or vanity and not to incite to sin often commit only venial sin; and since the things of the mind are concealed from us, we should not be too quick to judge the intentions of others.

Concerning what you have said about some women who powder and paint themselves and wear makeup in diverse colors, I cannot say what one should think of them. I remember that Suzanna, in the Old Testament, was molested by two perverse old men while she was washing at a fountain and awaiting the return of her servants whom she had sent to fetch her best and most perfumed lotions; she wished both to preserve her natural beauty and to please her husband.[60] It is true that Saint Augustine has written that women who wear makeup offend God, for not being content to be as God has made them, they desire to correct nature.[61] In keeping with that opinion, therefore, I should think that one shouldn't wear makeup, though I should think one might wear it with the right intention and not incur mortal sin. As Saint Thomas says (II, 2, question 9): "They are not committing mortal sin if they are not doing it out of arrogance, lasciviousness, or contempt of God; for there are times when one does it not to show or pretend to show beauty but to hide one's viciousness; and even when the action proceeds from some extrinsic or chance cause, because the real reasons are hidden from us, we must always accept these things in their best light."[62]

Therefore I beg you, don't be such a rash judge! I would suggest you begin to repent for having slandered those whom all good people endeavor to praise. For they realize that many women are deserving of eternal praise, among them Judith, of whom Saint Jerome said: "Take the woman Judith as an example of chastity and praise her with triumphal song and perpetual hymns and canticles. For He who rewarded her chastity made her worthy to be imitated not only by women but by men; and He so favored her that He gave her the strength to gain victory over an enemy who had until that time been invincible."[63]

O praiseworthy and excellent chastity, you have burned in many women's hearts like a constant flame! There are still a great many very noble ladies who kept the marriage bond with their gracious virtue, such as Arthemisia, the wife of Mansolus [sic]; Argia, the wife of Polimetes; Cornelia, the wife of Gracchus; and Hipsicrates, the wife of Mithridates. Others there are, too numerous to count, who preferred virginity to any other way of life—Atalanta, the virgin from Calidonia, who for the preservation of her maidenhood spent her days in the woods, forests, mountains and plains; Camilia, the Queen of the Vulcans, who exercised military discipline with a manly courage. How many women have valued virginity: Iphigenia, Cassandra, and Chryseis in Greece, to whose number one might add the virgins of Sparta, Mylesia, and Thebes. These women honor and ennoble the Hebrew and Greek histories, which tell us how they faced violent death rather than lose their virginity.[64]

Considering all this, I tend to think the plethora of your insults is unfounded. Many examples from history refute your inveterate ill-will; but that is not the only assistance I hope for. Many good men too will come to my aid, for reason will urge them to do so. I confess I am dumbfounded that you do not seem to fear the consequences that have befallen certain men who have spoken ill of women. Aren't you impressed by the punishment that Tiresias underwent for having said that the female sex was more lascivious than the male? This haughty and foolish

opinion deprived him of his sight.[65] Heavy too was the revenge which the goddess Ceres took on Erysichton for having despised her; if you remember correctly she reduced
him to such an extreme state of hunger that he ended up
eating himself.[66] Ajax, the son of Aiolus, who had shown
disrespect toward Minerva, also got what he deserved.[67]

I could cite other examples, but I shall refrain from
doing so as I fear that merely remonstrating with you
would not be enough to root out your wretched opinions. I
shall therefore give my tired pen a rest and pray God that
He may liberate you from your obstinate opinions.

FOURTH INVECTIVE LETTER

Shown by Lady Helisenne to Elenot, who with an arrogant and assiduous presumption has been assailing
women who want to dedicate themselves to literature. To dissuade him from this mad opinion Helisenne reminds him that there have been famous
women with brilliant and refined minds.

SINCE I BEGAN considering your arrogant and haughty
words to me I have simply come to the conclusion that
you have gone mad. You say you are convinced that you
are more knowledgeable than words can say, conception
fathom, or fantasy imagine. I pray, tell me: does your presumptuousness dazzle, becloud or otherwise blind you? In-
tellectually you seem to consider yourself as a product of
thundering Zeus's brain, which, as you know, brought
forth Athena, goddess of fortitude and prudence.[68]

I hold it beyond doubt that you are so imbued with

yourself that you think yourself more intelligent than those sisters who lived at the fountain of Pegasus.[69] I'm sure that if you really wanted to say openly what your wild imagination is thinking, you would probably blurt out that you outdo Clio in history, Melpomene in tragedy, Thalia in comedy, Euterpe in music, Terpsichore in dance, Erato in geometry [sic], Calliope in literature, Urania in astronomy, and Polimia in rhetoric.[70] You seem to think that Homer's glory as prince of poets and Herodotus as historian would have been even greater if they had talked and written about you; but then I'm sure you think that the Creator decided not to endow the early ages of the world with a figure so worthy of praise as you, for fear he would be depriving the later ages; hence you are sad only because you, a self-styled phoenix of wit and wisdom,[71] cannot uncover any poets or historiographers who are willing to sing your praises. One presumes that you would like the son of Phoebus and Coronis to come back to this planet so that he might agree, at your instigation, to resurrect the most learned men of ancient times and put them in your service.[72]

All this presumptuousness would ordinarily make me laugh, to be sure, were it not that in straining, as you do, to raise yourself up, you make it a point to bring others completely down. You inveigh against womankind in particular, and speaking in general terms, you say that women are rough and benighted people; and you conclude that their one and only pastime should be to spin.[73] I admire the haste with which you come to this conclusion. I have good reason to believe that if things were left up to you, you would deny women the privilege of pursuing literature, as they are incapable (so you say) of writing well.

If you were better read your opinion would be different. If your hostility toward women were not constantly nourished by inveterate ill-will, you would be less indifferent to the praise of women which adorns the pages of many a great orator. Quintilian did not hesitate to write that the literary skills of the daughters of Lelius and Hortensius (both very famous orators) made the elegant style of their fathers singularly attractive. Pythagoras' daughter Damas was so expert in philosophy that after the Fates had recalled her father from this life she commented on the most obscure points of his maxims. Queen Zenobia was so instructed by Longinus the philosopher that she was named Ephinisa for her wide-ranging and brilliant knowledge of literary texts. (Nichomachus translated her sacred writings.) Deborah was so well-versed in Greek that, as we read in the Book of Judges, she exercised the office of magistrate over the people of Israel. We also read in the Book of Judges that Queen Athalia reigned and judged seven years in Jerusalem. Cornelia, the mother of the Gracchi, taught them eloquence. Valeria, a Roman virgin, was so well versed in Greek and Latin literature that she explicated Virgil's metrics and verses in the light of the mysteries of the Christian faith. Aspasia was filled with such great knowledge that Socrates did not blush at learning anything from her, and this was attested by Pythian Apollo. Alpaides, a virgin and nun, was so filled with divine grace that the meaning of the books of the Bible was revealed to her. Areste, a woman of great erudition, was the mother of Aristippus the philosopher, whom she instructed in philosophy from his youth onward. Istrina, wife to King Aripithus of Scythia, taught the Greek literature to her son Salem. Sosipatra was so brilliant in poetic knowledge that the Ethics said she had been nurtured by the gods. There have also been great women poets and orators too: Capiola, Lucera, Sappho, and Armisia, surnamed Androginea.[74] I am convinced that whoever would accept to sail over the sea of great women of science and to list and talk about their works would spend more time navigating than Ulysses ever did in his painful wanderings.

But if you wretchedly persist in your objections, claiming that I mention nothing but antiquity and that there are no comparable woman writers nowadays, I would simply answer that you are wrong. For I believe that never was there in the past, nor will there ever be in the future, a loftier or more brilliant spirit than the most illustrious and distinguished princess, the queen of Navarre.[75] It is a fact widely acclaimed that her royal and lofty person combines Plato's godlike wisdom, Cato's prudence, Cicero's eloquence, and Socrates' wisdom. Her sincerity is so accomplished, in short, that her brilliance enhances all of womankind; her example alone is enough to refute your vain and futile opinions. I thing it is high time you silence your corrosive, infernal tongue.

But silence does not come easily to you. It is obvious that you are addicted to the loathsome vice of slander. I can recall, in fact, that on one occasion when your appetite for despising women was not satisfied, you were obliged to follow your natural inclination and slander men. Among them were men so respected that even if your life were not as durable as that of old Nestor, however hard you were to try, you could never be worthy enough to carry their books behind them. O how sad am I when I recall the memory of your unnecessarily harsh words! Yet it is imperative that I recall what you said, otherwise my wounded heart could never unburden itself.

I am sure you remember how your venomous tongue, mouthing wretched lies, attempted to downgrade the high, sweet style of that most eloquent poet Marot, whose works are so elegant and so outstanding that kings and princes delight in them.[76] At first I didn't know what I should think of you; but after thoughtful consideration, I am convinced that the most apt thing one could compare you to is a ship filled with water or some other liquid that cannot help over-flowing. So it is with your wretched self, which is completely intoxicated and brimming with slander. It is easy enough to see that you are simply over-spilling with words, and I'll simply pay attention to you no longer.

A painful anxiety disturbs me, unfortunately, when I recall that you have let it be known with your loathsome, mincing words that you would like to spend time reading my *Angoysses*, one of my lesser compositions. This is quite contrary to my wishes, for I like my books to be shown to competent people. I know that some men of wit are naturally inclined to praise other people willingly, so that even if my works were of little value they would be kind enough to pardon the weakness of my style. I know that their encouragement would be a stimulus comparable to the one that impelled me to write in the first place, namely the fear I had of going under and drowning in the perilous sea of inactivity. Therefore I am reassured beyond doubt that they would enjoy reading my modest works and approve of them. What a boundless pleasure it is for me to think that my books are being published in this great city of Paris, which is filled with innumerable crowds of people who love science, elegance, leisure and culture—the graces that flow from conversing with Minerva.

The only thing that disturbs these pleasant thoughts is the annoyance I feel in considering that if perverse fortune allows one ignorant, dishonest, wicked person to exist in that great city and then allows my books to fall within that blind man's hands, I am sure he will give them an unfavorable review. For though my works are as nothing compared to the difficult publications that are proliferating daily, that man still won't have the ability to understand them. I know the incapacity of his mind; and since it is easy to misjudge what one doesn't understand, it doesn't augur well that he is my critic, and I have little hope of avoiding the perilous lash of his tongue. O unhappy creature! You ought to know that if the days of the great metamorphoses were still with us, a loathsome person like you would risk undergoing the punishment of Midas, that unhappy king whose beastliness made him grow such long ears.[77] What would you do if your rash and foolish judgment were to lead you to a similar fate? Think of the trouble you would have hiding your monstrous ears!

Midas' example, surely, should make you apprehensive enough to close your shameful mouth, restrain your venomous tongue and beg mercy of these people whom you have so gravely offended. If you were willing to root out the perversity in you, I would persuade all women to forgive you. I am sure none of them would refuse such a request, as they are naturally inclined to be urbane, sweet, and forgiving. Aristotle bears out this point when he writes that women are easily moved to mercy and pity and are therefore easily inclined to forgive as they know there is nothing more apt to make life more enjoyable than the forgiveness of past injuries. This tendency corroborates the natural goodness of women, which I have mentioned to you before; so don't despair of becoming reconciled with them. Why don't you seriously consider a public admission of the offense you have done to the gracious female sex, which the Church itself calls devout? If you succeed in doing so, as I urge you to, you will feel better. Reason calls for it, honesty consents to it, conscience ordains it.

I should very much like you to pass on this letter of mine to a few sound-minded, intelligent people; surely, once having read it, they would enable you to understand that if I am remonstrating with you, it is for your own good. But should you choose to hide my letter, I fear that, lacking good advice, you will persist in your usual madness; this would only serve to release the fury of my pen and make me write things more irritating than you could possibly predict.

With these words I shall bring the present letter to a close, imploring the Lord of Heaven to enlighten your benighted judgment with His special grace.

FIFTH INVECTIVE LETTER

Lady Helisenne to the inhabitants of a small town, who were ill-natured beyond belief.

SINCE I HAVE LEARNED, gentlemen citizens of Icvoc, that you feel I am to be blamed because in my writings I recorded the smallest portion of your usual crimes, I have spent some time delving quietly into my thoughts, thinking over my narration of some of your natural vices. I have done so in order to determine whether I have deserved any of the blame ascribed to me. But having thought it over thoroughly and wishing to render a just judgment, I blame myself exceedingly for having committed a great fault: at the time I started to publicize the detestable way you live, I should have ascertained whether or not my style was capable of exposing and publicizing the extreme perversity of your way of life.

Unfortunately, if I had thought matters over, my mind would have convinced me that it was not in my power to express anything so vile. O unreflecting and too hasty judgment of mine! The mere memory of which makes me sad! I fear that the people who enjoyed reading my writings did not realize the excessive nature of your obvious criminal acts. Had they realized that I set out to write something which was not within my power to carry through, they would have been able to reproach me. Therefore I cannot imagine what valid excuse I could invent in response to such a reproach unless I say that when I undertook this task my pen was not yet accustomed to expressing invectives. Since this was a new and unaccustomed thing for me, it was my opinion that I had exposed enough of your criminal acts. But now that I know the contrary, I would like to amend my silence concerning your iniquities, and publish the slander produced by your venomous tongues. To begin with, let me say that as far as you are concerned, vice is virtue, modesty is incontinence, fraud is faith, betrayal is innocence, and furor is mercy.

Furthermore, idleness, which consumes you with malice, is extremely dangerous; as you recall, it spurred Aegisthus to commit adultery and homicide.[78] Being submerged in vicious idleness, you surprisingly go even beyond Epicurean pleasures, claiming Venus, Bacchus, Ceres as your earthly gods. Keeping these things in mind, it is easy to realize that idleness accompanied by voluptuousness is responsible for creating the vices that smear you with perpetual infamy. These have accumulated in your wretched persons more than any fluent tongue can say. However, I shall stop generalizing about your collective vices and address myself to one of you who exceeds and outdoes the others in all the vices, especially in that of treason. I would name him, but I presume that the superabundance of his wicked deeds has been publicized far and wide. Hence, if I call him the most wicked of you all, there will be no one so dimwitted as to fail to recognize him. In order to point him out, I want to say that though he is old in wickedness, he is rather young in years. Though it is certain that he has not yet reached the age beyond which all correction is impossible, it is true that from his adolescent years until his thirtieth year (his present age), he has spent all his time perpetuating innumerable evil deeds. Surrounded by an infinite variety of vices, he leads a wicked, detestable, and miserable life. Despite his young age, such a life, being so hardened to evil, cannot be corrected. As Quintilian says, one can more easily break than correct the man who is given over to evil.[79] This is why one should not think it possible for wretches to reform.

Realizing this, I can justly say to him, the most wicked among you: O damned, and more than damned, evil, wicked, false pretender! O wicked traitor, who could deny that within yourself all deceptions, frauds, and collusions are lodged? It is clear that you never give up knowing how to veil truth with lies, and color lies with truth. I don't know who your childhood mentors were; but remembering the subtle deceptions of Ulysses, and the betrayal of Anthenor, one can easily presume that you tore a leaf from their book.[80] For most certainly you are a true and exemplary imitator of theirs, and for this reason to keep company with you is no less an infamy than it is a shame. Realizing this, I was most irritated when I learned of your visit to the great city of Paris. It is not seemly for you to converse with such honest people as the Parisians. Since then, I have been informed of the venomous slander with which you attempted to contaminate several people. But when you had said so much about them that nothing else presented itself to your false fantasy, you began to probe further within your bag of slander, wishing to know if it were so dried out and arid that nothing else could come out of it. And after spending some time in this natural exercise you still found a potion which you intended for me, not knowing, however, what else to say except that my book entitled *Angoysses* was too intelligible, and that I should have spoken in a more veiled manner, without designating specific places. Of course I understand what made you say such things; in reading my books, you and your other friends had understood that I make reference to your crude and wicked treatment of the most gracious knights Guenelic and Quezinstra.[81] I can see that having carried out your iniquities, you would prefer that they be passed over in silence, so that distant regions would not be made aware of them.

But I assure you that the more you try to hide your vices, the more publicized they will be. Believe me, if you, the most wicked inhabitant of this town, had spent a long time in Paris, the noble citizens of that great city would have had sure evidence of your detestable life because of their subtle and splendid minds. I know, without a doubt, that like the good laborer, who is used to pulling out the weeds from his garden, they would have expelled you from such a place of which you are unworthy; and therefore you have done well to leave before such shame befell you. I hear that now you are reduced to the company of your evil colleagues, of whom you are certainly the prince. This is my final word, as I don't want to write anything more, except to assure you of my desire to see you old, crippled, blind, deaf, mute, indigent, and destitute. If Atropos cuts the thread of your miserable life because you do not have in you the strength to tolerate such calamities, I hope that your body will remain unburied, that it will become a prey for leopards, famished wolves, lions, bears, tigers, and all ferocious beasts, who will satisfy their violent hunger on you.

With this wish, I shall end my letter; as not to forget your companions, tell them I hope that what befell Dathan and Abiram[82] will befall them as well.

Here end the Personal and Invective
Letters of Lady Helisenne, composed
by her: Printed in Paris by Denys Janot.

End page of the 1539 edition of the letters, published by Denys Janot.

NOTES ON THE TEXT

1. Helisenne's publisher, Denys Janot, had printed *Les Angoysses douloureuses* a year earlier (1538). His request for permission to publish "two little volumes," *Les Epistres familieres et invectives* and *Le Songe* is accompanied by a plea that no other bookdealer or printer be allowed to sell Helisenne's works under pain of confiscation. Janot's letter gives some idea of the popularity which *Les Angoysses* must have enjoyed.

2. By calling upon Plato's authority and God's assistance, Helisenne sets the tone which she retains throughout *Les Epistres*: her Christian sources are paralleled by references to works by pagan authors.

3. Known in mythology for his great age, Nestor is depicted in the *Iliad* as a kind old man, fond of giving ineffective and unnecessary advice. (*See Iliad*, I, v. 247 ff; II, v. 75 ff; X, v. 204 ff; XXII, v. 306 ff.)

4. Reputed for her chastity, Suzanna was falsely accused of adultery by two lascivious elders and was saved from being stoned to death by the young Daniel (Daniel 13:1−64). See note 60.

5. An approximate version of this anecdote is related by Diogenes Laertes, "Socrates," II, 35, in *Lives of Eminent Philosophers*, translated by R.D. Hicks, 2 vols., The Loeb Classical Library (Cambridge, Mass.: Harvard University Press, 1925; rpt. 1959), I, 165. Helisenne may have been acquainted with the original of the *Lives*, as the work was translated into Latin (1431) and subsequently published in Rome (c.1475), Venice (1475, 1490, 1497), twice in Paris (n.d.), and Basel (1524) in addition to publications in the original Greek (1533) and Italian (1480, 1488, and 1494). On the other hand, she might have encountered this anecdote in Christine de Pisan's *Le Livre de la cité des dames*, II, 21, 1. Perhaps she is using a secondary source for this whole passage on friendship, fortune, and revenge.

6. Alain de Lille, a French philosopher, also known as "Alanus de Insulis" (c.1115−1202), was sometimes called "Doctor universalis" because of his great learning. Helisenne is probably referring here to a long passage on the mutability of Fortune in Alanus' major work, *Anticlaudianus*; see Alanus de Insulis, *Anticlaudianus*, VIII, in *Patrologiae Cursus Completus Opera Omnia*, edited by J.D. Migne (Paris: Petit-Montrouge, 1855), 210, 559−61; c.f. Fritz Neubert's discussions of Helisenne's sources, "Antike und Christentum bei den ersten franzö-

sischen Epistoliers der Renaissance, Helisenne de Crenne und Estienne du Tronchet (1539 und 1569)," *Romanische Forschungen* 77 (1965): 1–41; and "Die französischen Briefschreiber der Renaissance und ihre Verleger," *Germanisch-Romanische Monatsschrift* 49, n.18 (1968): 349–60.

7. The Roman politician and writer Cassiodorus (c.490–c.580), known for his encyclopedic knowledge, founded a religious community at Vivarum, in Calabria, where he established the practice of copying ancient manuscripts. Among his works, *Institutiones divinarum et saecularium litterarum* was the most influential. Helisenne is probably referring here to a lost commentary of Cassiodorus on the *Epistle to the Romans*.

8. King David is known as "The Psalmist" because about seventy-three psalms are attributed to him. Helisenne is probably paraphrasing Psalm 55 (Vulgate 54):23: "men of blood and treachery shall not live out half their days"; Psalm 5:6: "the Lord abhors bloodthirsty and deceitful men"; and perhaps Proverbs 6:16–17: "There are six things which the Lord hates. . . . hands that shed innocent blood." Unless stated otherwise these and all subsequent Biblical references are to *The Holy Bible*, Revised Standard Version (London: Oxford University Press, 1962).

9. A skillful craftsman, designer, and architect, Daedalus was especially known for the labyrinth he constructed in Crete to house the Minotaur. While in Crete, he also made the famous thread for Ariadne, and a small wooden statue of Venus, to which Helisenne is alluding (see note 34).

10. According to Greek legend, the Athenian hero Theseus was sent to Crete in order to slay the Minotaur. He managed to do so thanks to the help given him by Ariadne, daughter of the King of Crete. After seducing her and taking her away from Crete, he abandoned her on the island of Naxos and married her sister Phaedra (see Ovid, *Heroides*, X). The mythological women mentioned by Helisenne in this passage are found both in Ovid and in later literature; it is therefore difficult to determine whether Helisenne was basing herself on Ovid or on other sources. Most of these "abandoned" women are mentioned in such works as *Le Roman de la rose*; Boccaccio's *De claris mulieribus* and *Fiammetta* (translated into French from Italian in 1535, a definite source of Helisenne's *Angoysses*) and Christine de Pisan's *Le Livre de la cité des dames*. Ovid's *Heroides* were very popular in Helisenne's time, judging from the numerous editions; there were at least eight Latin edi-

tions printed in France and Italy between 1471 and 1538; Helisenne may have known one of these, but it appears more likely that she was using a most interesting (though undated) French translation, *Le Recueil des espistres d'Ovide translaté en françoys o vray ligne pour ligne, faisans mencion de cinq loyalles amoureuses* . . . Four of the "cinq loyalles amoureuses" are mentioned in this very passage: Zenone (Oenone), Adryane (Ariadne), Philis (Phyllis), and Ysiphile (Hypsipyle). Dido is mentioned later (Eighth Letter, note 25). It is significant that no other heroines are mentioned by Helisenne except these.

11. Paris, youngest and most handsome son of the Trojan King Priam, loved and married the river nymph Oenone, but abandoned her when given the chance to carry off Helen, Queen of Sparta, thus precipitating the Trojan war. In the fifth epistle of Ovid's *Heroides*, Oenone writes to Paris, reproaching him bitterly and asserting that she is still his faithful wife (see note 10).

12. During his journey back home to Athens after the Trojan war, Demophon, son of Theseus, spent some time in Thrace where Princess Phyllis fell in love with him. He continued his journey home after promising to return to her. Despairing of his coming, she hanged herself and was turned into an almond tree, which flowered when Demophon finally returned (see Ovid, *Heroides*, II, and note 10).

13. Jason spent two years with Hypsipyle, Queen of Lemnos, as lover and promised husband, before his marriage to Medea. In Ovid (*Heroides*, VI), she writes Jason a reproachful letter after hearing of his flight with Medea and the Golden Fleece.

14. Helisenne's quote is an approximate version of the following: "For the wrongdoers will soon fade like the grass, and wither like the green herb" (Psalm 37 [Vulgate 36]:2).

15. The source of this specific quotation is unknown. Socrates often refers to his poverty with regard to material possessions in order to emphasize the importance of non-material values. One such discourse is found in Xenophon, *Memorabilia*, in *Xenophon in Seven Volumes: IV, Memorabilia and Oeconomicus*, translated by E.C. Marchant, *Symposium and Apology*, translated by O.J. Todd, The Loeb Classical Library (Cambridge, Mass.: Harvard University Press, 1923; rpt. 1968), Book I, ii, 5–7 (p.15).

16. Helisenne is quoting directly from Cicero, *Paradoxa Stoicorum*, I, 8: "Omnia mecum porto mea." See Cicero, *De Oratore* . . . *Together with De Fato etc.*, translated by H. Rackham, The Loeb Clas-

sical Library (Cambridge, Mass.: Harvard University Press, 1942; rpt. 1960), p.261. She may have read the French translation, *Les Paradoxes*, published by Denys Janot in 1539.

17. "I keep every lust and greed in check." Diogenes (c. 400–325 B.C.) taught the importance of self-sufficiency and the reduction of bodily needs to a minimum. He is better known for his originality in applying his philosophy to everyday life than for his philosophical theories themselves. For the account of Diogenes' encounter with Alexander, see Plutarch, *Alexander*, in *Plutarch's Lives in Eleven Volumes, Demosthenes and Cicero, Alexander and Caesar*, translated by Bernadotte Perrin, The Loeb Classical Library (Cambridge, Mass.: Harvard University Press, 1919; rpt. 1958), vol. VII, p.259.

18. "Look at the birds in the air: they neither sow nor reap nor gather into barns, and yet your heavenly Father feeds them" (Matthew 6:26).

19. Both Marcus Varro, writer and commentator (116–27 B.C.), and Servius, grammarian and commentator (fourth century A.D.), compared the six ages of the world to the ages of man. See P. Archambault, "The Ages of Man and the Ages of the World," *Etudes Augustiniennes* 11, no. 3–4 (Fall 1966): 193–224.

20. Plato uses this and similar expressions in several works. See especially *Republic*, VII 518b–519.

21. Matthew 7:7.

22. Samuel 12:14–23.

23. The politician, poet, and scientist Empedocles (c. 493–443 B.C.), native of Agrigento, was so greatly admired for his knowledge and wisdom that it is said he thought himself divine. According to one unverified account (retold by Diogenes Laertius, "Empedocles," VIII, 69, in *Lives of Eminent Philosophers*, II, 383, 385), he jumped into the volcano Etna during an eruption, perhaps to prove his divinity.

24. In the fourth century B.C., Marcus Curtius sacrificed his life by plunging into a deep chasm which suddenly opened in the Forum, thus proving his patriotism and bravery. The officiating priest had declared that the chasm would remain opened unless a Roman citizen voluntarily jumped in. This myth helped explain the name of "Lacus Curtius," designating a pit in the Roman Forum. It is likely that Helisenne read this story in Saint Augustine, *City of God*, V, 18.

25. Daughter of a king of Tyre, Dido founded and became queen of Carthage, after the murder of her husband (see Virgil, *Aeneid*, I, vv. 340 ff.; IV, vv. 117 ff.; and Ovid, *Heroides*, VII).

26. Helisenne makes almost no references to Christian or Classical examples in her tenth letter, the most startlingly personal of the collection. It is evident that in those letters that seem derived from deeply felt personal experiences she uses almost no literary maxims or exempla.

27.Helisenne is making an allusion to the underworld, to the watchdog Cerberus, and to the three Fates: Clotho spun the thread of life, Lachesis measured it, and Atropos cut it.

28. The young god Hyacinthus was accidently killed by a discus hurled by his lover Apollo. Griefstricken, Apollo caused a flower bearing this name to spring from the dead god's blood.

29. In *Les Angoysses douloureuses*, Quezinstra is the name of the faithful friend and companion of Helisenne's lover, Guenelic.

30. The source of this specific reference is unknown; it is not found in Plutarch's *Alexander*. Among treatises dealing with friendship, Helisenne may have drawn, in general, on Cicero's *De amicitia*, published by Denys Janot in 1539 as part of *Les Oeuvres* (2: *Livre de amytie*), and on Xenophon's *Memorabilia*, especially Book II, iv, 1, where Socrates claims "that of all possessions the most precious is a good and sincere friend" (see *Xenophon in Seven Volumes*, IV, *Memorabilia*, p. 123).

31. The ninth chapter of Proverbs, in which Wisdom and Folly are personified as hostesses, does not contain this maxim. Throughout the book of Proverbs, one finds the themes of justice and prudence intertwined with friendship (e.g., 18:34, 19:14, 27:10). Perhaps Helisenne had one of these in mind.

32. Helisenne appears to be addressing her lover; she seems to be imprisoned and carefully guarded by two guards delegated by her husband. It is evident that she is using the term "castle" both literally and figuratively: as the place of her imprisonment and, in keeping with the courtly love tradition, as a symbol for her "surrendered" self.

33. In mythology, the monster Argus was known to be an excellent watchman because of his hundred eyes. Upon an order from Zeus, Hermes (Mercury) managed to put him to sleep by telling him the story of Syrinx and Pan as boringly as he could. Argus' eyes closed one by

one, and Hermes slew him. Throughout this letter, Helisenne uses this name to refer, cryptically, to the person who is guarding her, perhaps her husband or more likely the person(s) delegated by him.

34. Scylla betrayed her father Nisus, King of Megara, by cutting off his one red hair, on which his power depended. According to Ovid (*Metamorphoses*, VIII, vv. 1–152), she was motivated by her all-consuming love for Minos, King of Crete. Minos was horrified that she should have thus betrayed her father and set sail, leaving her on the shore. She threw herself into the sea in order to follow him, and as she gripped the stern of his vessel, she was changed forever into a bird. At least ten editions of the *Metamorphoses* appeared, in French and Latin, between 1479 and 1539. Helisenne probably had access to the French translation of 1539, published by her own editor, Denys Janot.

35. Daedalus, the master craftsman and architect, manufactured wings for himself and his son Icarus, so that they could fly away from Crete, where they were imprisoned by King Minos. He used wax to attach the wings to their bodies, and instructed Icarus to fly low, so as to avoid the intense heat of the sun. Carried away by enthusiasm, Icarus flew too high, the sun melted the wax, and Icarus was plunged into the sea, where he drowned (see Ovid, *Metamorphoses*, VIII, vv. 182–235).

36. Phaeton, son of Apollo, received Apollo's reluctant permission to drive the sun chariot for one day, but lost control of the "swift horses" and found himself and the chariot of fire hurtling to earth. The intense heat charred certain parts of the earth, scorching the skins of the Ethiopians.

37. The Greek hero of the Trojan war, Achilles, son of Thetis, was beside himself with grief when his closest friend, Patroclus, died in battle (see *Iliad*, XVIII, vv. 18–36; 314–56).

38. The allegorical figure of Rumor, often represented with wings and blowing a trumpet, was the messenger of Jupiter. According to Virgil (*Aeneid*, IV, vv. 173–97, 298–99), she was born in order to denounce the crimes of the gods.

39. After ten years of war against the Greeks, Priam, King of Troy, lived to see his many children die and his kingdom fall to the enemy.

40. In Greek mythology, the monster Scylla devoured men, whereas the whirlpool Charybdis sank ships; they were located opposite each other in the Strait of Messina (she is not the same Scylla as in note 34).

41. Helisenne's reference seems incorrect. In *City of God*, III, 18, Saint Augustine does mention a temple on the banks of the Tiber, but it is consecrated to Vesta, not to the Goddess Fortune. The latter is mentioned, however, in other parts of his work, such as IV, 9 and 18; and VII, 3. Helisenne appears to rely on her memory when referring to Saint Augustine's and to Saint Jerome's works (note 58), which accounts for her inaccuracies.

42. As told by Ovid (*Metamorphoses*, IV, 56–165), Piramus, the most beautiful youth, and Thisbe, the loveliest maid of all the East, loved each other but were forbidden by their parents to meet. The force of their love was such that they planned to elope despite their parents' disapproval and decided to meet by a crystal fountain. The inadvertent arrival of a lioness was the cause of their death; Piramus killed himself, thinking Thisbe had been the lioness' victim. Thisbe then arrived, and seeing her lover dead, also committed suicide.

43. The vestal virgin Claudia had been accused of corruption. In order to prove her innocence, she pulled a boat containing a statue of the goddess Vesta all the way from Phrygia to Rome by means of a slight cord, even though all previous efforts had been unable to budge it. Helisenne might have encountered this story in Plutarch's *De virtutibus mulierum* (translated by Almanus Ranutinus, in Jean Tixier's *De memorabilibus et claris mulieribus*, published in 1521). A variant of this anecdote, ascribed to Boccaccio, is found in Christine de Pisan's *Le Livre de la cité des dames*, II, 63.1. Helisenne's ascribed source, Philometor, remains unidentified.

44. Helisenne's reference is correct here. In *City of God*, XXII, 11, Augustine relates this "miracle," as told by Varro, about the Vestal virgin who proved her chastity by carrying water in a sieve. He suggests that if this is the work of a god, how much more can the all powerful God, the creator of the world, be capable of.

45. Juno, wife of Jupiter, King of the Gods, was worshipped as the patroness of married women.

46. The style of this letter seems to indicate that the husband's "reply" was written by Helisenne herself. Attributing the letter to her husband enables her to formulate characteristic antifeminist arguments.

47. Odysseus' wife Penelope is known for her wisdom and faithfulness, as shown by her exemplary conduct during the twenty years that she awaited his return from Troy.

48. According to various legends, Semiramis, ruler of Assyria after the death of her husband, King Ninus, was known not only for her

military prowess and for building Babylon, but also for the incestuous love she bore her own son. These diverse legends seem to be founded on the historical personage Sammouramat, queen and regent of Assyria in the ninth century, *B.C.*

49. Socrates' wife, Xanthippe, was notoriously ill-tempered. The source of this specific quotation is unknown. It is not found in Xenophon's *Memorabilia* or Diogenes Laertius' "Socrates," though Diogenes Laertius does refer to her as a "shrew" (see *Lives of Eminent Philosophers*, I, 167).

50. Helisenne lists a series of couples, in which the women are reputed, not always justly, to have caused the misfortune of the men who loved them. She is probably using a compilation as source material, for this type of list was often found in antifeminist works of this period, beginning with Jean de Meung's *Le Roman de la rose*, and including such treatises as Gratien DuPont's *Controverses des sexes masculin et femenin* (1534). Among Helisenne's examples are the following: Cleopatra, who betrayed her husband and ally, Mark Anthony, according to some accounts, either at the battle of Actium, or upon Octavian's subsequent arrival in Egypt; Samson, known for his superhuman strength, who was defeated by the Philistines after being seduced and betrayed by Delilah; Philip, King of Macedonia, who was assassinated by Pausanias, but his wife, Olimpias, was held responsible; Agrippina, mother of the Roman emperor Nero, known for having poisoned her husband Claudius, and killed upon Nero's orders in 59 *B.C.*

51. Note the scholastic tone of Helisenne's argumentation here. Helisenne turns her husband's use of terms like *generalement* and *condition* against him: if Socrates railed against the whole category of women one must remember that he too belonged to a category, that of henpecked husbands.

52. Proverbs 5:3–6, 20, and 6: 23–26.

53. Proverbs 31:10–31.

54. Lucretia, wife of Tarquinius Collatinus, is known for her great chastity, for she chose to commit suicide after being raped by Sextus, son of the last king of Rome, Tarquinius Sextus, in 509 *B.C.* Helisenne's source could be Saint Augustine, *City of God*, I, 19, where Augustine mentions chaste women whose honor has been violated.

55. Deuteronomy 21:10–14.

56. Helisenne is perhaps thinking of Genesis 24:21: "The man gazed at her in silence to learn whether the Lord had prospered his journey or not."

57. The beautiful and intelligent Abigail saved her husband Nabal from young David's wrath by giving David a peace offering; shortly after, her husband died and King David married her (see 1 Samuel 25:14–42).

58. Father of the Church and revisor and translator of the Vulgate Bible, Saint Jerome (c. 347–420) was very influential in shaping Church doctrines and attitudes. Among his letters are several addressed to women, especially virgins and widows, in which he exhorts them to retain their chastity. The most famous of these letters is the one to Eustochium (22) in praise of virginity. He also discusses the importance of apparel and adornments with relation to a chaste life in his letters to Marcella (38), to Laeta (107), to a mother and her daughter (117), and to Pacatula (128). It is difficult to know which of Jerome's letters Helisenne is paraphrasing. See Saint Jerome, *Select Letters*, translated by F.A. Wright, The Loeb Classical Library (Cambridge, Mass.: Harvard University Press, 1954).

59. Proverbs 7:10 and *passim*.

60. See also note 4. Suzanna and Judith (note 63) are both examples of Biblical heroines who exemplify Helisenne's precept that a woman may show herself to best advantage by using fine oils and perfumes (such as Suzanna) and wearing becoming clothing (Judith) and yet retain her virtue.

61. Saint Augustine, in a letter to his friend Possidius, expresses several interesting notions on makeup and ornaments; although he considers some uses of makeup as sinful, he by no means condemns ornaments in general. (See Saint Augustine, *Select Letters*, translated by James Houston Baxter, The Loeb Classical Library [Cambridge, Mass.: Harvard University Press, 1930; rpt. 1965], Ep. 245, p. 479 ff.) Passages from this letter are quoted and commented upon by Saint Thomas, *Summa Theologica* (see note 62).

62. Helisenne's correct reference to Saint Thomas' *Summa Theologica* is an adaptation of the original: "Non tamen semper talis fucatio est cum peccato mortali: sed solum quando fit propter lasciviam, vel in Dei contemptum. . . . Sciendum tamen quod aliud est fingere pulchritudinem non habitam: et aliud est occultare turpitudinem ex aliqua causa provenientem."

63. The Biblical heroine Judith was a brave young widow who saved her people, the Israelites, from the Assyrian enemy by visiting their general, Holophernes, in his tent, and cutting off his head after he had fallen asleep. Helisenne's reference is to Saint Jerome's Preface

to the Book of Judith (*Patrologiae Cursus Completus*, edited by J.D. Migne [Paris: Petit-Montrouge, 1865], 29, col. 41–42): "Accipite Judith viduam, castitatis exemplum, et triumphali laude, perpetuis eam praeconiis declarate. Hanc enim non solum feminis, sed et viris imitabilem dedit, qui castitatis ejus remunerator virtutem ei talem tribuit, ut invictum omnibus hominibus vinceret, et insuperabilem superaret." In his treatise on the superiority of women, *De nobilitate et praecellentia foeminei sexus* (1529), Cornelius Agrippa refers to Judith as one of these women who, though they have performed criminal deeds, are praised rather than condemned for them.

    64. Helisenne's principal source for this passage is the short work in praise of women by Cornelius Agrippa, *De nobilitate et praecellentia foeminei sexus* (1529; translated into French in 1530: *Déclamation de la noblesse et préexcellence du sexe féminin*). I have used a later edition, *De l'excellence et de la supériorité de la femme* (Paris: Imprimerie Delance, 1801), which is conveniently divided into chapters and pages.

    In the second half of the book (pp. 60–65 of the 1801 edition), Agrippa gives many Biblical examples of men who were the first to commit specific sins and crimes (such as Adam, Cain, and Noah); after listing the many men who committed fornication and adultery, he goes on to say that with rare exceptions, women are known for their chastity and continence, whether they are married or not. All of the women named by Helisenne are listed by Agrippa in just about the same order. These are examples culled from ancient history and mythology: Arthemisia, wife and sister of Mausoleus (spelled Mansolus by Helisenne and other contemporary writers), satrap of Caria, who built a funeral monument for her husband after his death in 353 B.C., which was one of the seven wonders of the ancient world and is the source of our word "mausoleum"; Argia, wife of Polimetes of Thebes; Cornelia, daughter of the Roman general, Scipio, known not only for her devotion to her husband Tiberius Gracchus, but for raising and personally supervising the education of her two sons, known as the "Gracchi," after his death; Hipsicrates, the wife of Mithridates, King of Pontus; Atalanta of Calidonia, who would consider marrying only a suitor more fleetfooted than she; Camilia, daughter of the King of the Vulcans, who was brought up by her father to enjoy hunting and died in battle. The three girls Iphigenia, Cassandra, and Chryseis, are all connected with the war between the Greek states and Troy. They were each, in various ways, used as pawns by the men who determined the course of the war. Iphigenia, daughter of Agamemnon, King of Mycenae, was sacrificed, while yet a virgin, to the gods in exchange for favorable winds to enable the Greek army to leave for Troy; Cassandra, the daughter of Priam, King of Troy, though she was loved by Apollo, preferred to keep her virginity; Chryseis, daughter of the priest of Apollo, was the reluctant and much disputed captive of Agamemnon.

65. According to one of several legends, the Theban Tiresias was changed into a woman, and later back into a man. Because of this unique experience of bisexuality, he was asked by Hera and Zeus to resolve their argument as to which of the two sexes is better able to enjoy sexual pleasure. He immediately decided in favor of women. Hera was furious at this, feeling he was thus revealing Woman's secret, and blinded him. Zeus partially compensated for this by bestowing upon him the gift of prophecy.

66. Erysichton had the reputation for scorning the gods; he went so far as to violate the sacred grove of Ceres by cutting down an ancient oak within it. Ceres decided he deserved an atrocious punishment: he suffered hunger so extreme that nothing could satisfy it. He finally began to tear at and eat his own flesh, thus killing himself.

67. Ajax the Locrian is referred to as Ajax "son of Aiolus," in order to distinguish him from his fellow warrior and far greater hero, Ajax, son of Telamon. He brought upon his people a curse which lasted for many years because of his impious behavior during the fall of Troy. Having found the Trojan princess, Cassandra, seeking protection at the altar of the goddess Athena, he tore her away, along with the statue she was clinging to, in order to take possession of her. This grievous infraction of religious custom, and other acts of impiety, incurred the revenge of Athena against him and his people.

68. According to Greek mythology, Athena, goddess of wisdom, sprang from the head of Zeus, her father.

69. The Muses lived by a spring which had been formed when Pegasus, the winged horse, had struck the mountain, Helicon, with his hoof (see Ovid, *Metamorphoses*, V, v.255 ff.).

70. Daughters of Zeus and Mnemosyne, the Muses were personifications of artistic and intellectual pursuits, thus exemplifying the height of accomplishment in each field. Erato is usually identified with lyric and love poetry.

71. According to legend, the phoenix was a bird that would die, only to rise again from its ashes; figuratively, an outstanding, unique individual.

72. Asclepios, son of Phoebus (Apollo) and Coronis, was, according to Homer, expert in the art of healing and even reviving the dead. He gradually came to be much honored as the god of medicine.

73. This image is probably based on Proverbs 31:19. It is also found in Cornelius Agrippa's *De l'excellence et de la superiorité de la femme*, p. 96 (see also note 64).

74. This long passage in praise of wise and learned women closely resembles one in Cornelius Agrippa's *De nobilitate et praecellentia foeminei sexus*. Agrippa mentions all but three names (Alpaides, Areste and Sosipatra) and comments upon several more than once (see *De l'excellence . . .*, ch. 21–23, pp. 73–82). Such compiled lists of accomplished women are readily found in treatises of this period, especially in those dealing with the Querelle des Femmes. Jean Tixier's *De memorabilibus et claris mulieribus*, printed in 1521, includes several profeminist works, plus a very long catalogue of outstanding women, totaling about 200 names. Helisenne uses this assortment of names to lead up to the name of the queen of Navarre, whom she praises highly in the next passage.

75. Marguerite (1492–1549), queen of Navarre and sister of King Francis I of France, was not only an important patroness of the arts but author of several works, the best known of which is the *Heptameron*, a collection of seventy-two tales told in the manner of Boccaccio. This paragraph of fulsome praise indicates that Helisenne may have welcomed the queen's protection. If the two women writers knew each other, there is no document to prove it, despite claims to the contrary made by Hyacinthe Dusevel, *Lettres sur le département de la Somme* (Amiens, 1827), pp. 72–73; cf. *Biographie des hommes célèbres . . . du département de la Somme* (Amiens: Machart, 1835), pp. 209–11, quoted in Antonio Possenti, "Hélisenne de Crenne nel secolo dei Romantici e la prima conquista della critica," *Francia* 13 (January–March 1975): 30–32.

76. Known for his sonnets and his sympathy for Reformist thinkers, Clément Marot (1496–1544) was one of the poets who enjoyed the patronage of Marguerite de Navarre. Denys Janot published Marot's works in 1538; Helisenne may be referring to Marot's French translation of Erasmus' work in favor of educated women, *Colloque de l'abbé et de la femme savante*.

77. During a musical competition between Marsyas (Pan) and Apollo, Midas, king of Phrygia, was the only person present who found

Marsyas to be the better musician. Apollo retaliated by changing his ears into those of an ass, thus symbolizing his lack of finesse and discretion. See Ovid, *Metamorphoses*, XI, v.92 ff.

78. Aegisthus was the lover of Clytemnestra and the murderer of her husband, Agamemnon, king of Myceneae, after the latter's return from Troy. Ovid, in *Remedia amoris*, links Aegisthus' adultery to his idleness.

79. Helisenne probably has in mind Quintilian's basic precept, which defines an orator as a "good man": "Vir bonus dicendi peritus." He adds that it is almost impossible to "correct" an evil man. (See Quintilian, *Institutio oratoria*, XII, 1.)

80. Ulysses and Anthenor were heroes of the Trojan War, both known for their deceptive ways.

81. The two knights-errant, Helisenne's lover Guenelic and his faithful companion Quezinstra, wander around until they find the captive Helisenne, in Books two and three of her first work, *Les Angoysses douloureuses*.

82. Abiram and Dathan formed a conspiracy against Moses and resisted his authority. Refusing to appear before him, they were swallowed up by the earth (Numbers 16:12–30). Helisenne longs for this punishment in *Les Angoysses douloureuses*, chapter 12, rather than submit to her jealous husband's wrath.

BIBLIOGRAPHY

Sixteenth-Century Editions of *Les Epistres familieres et invectives*

these seven editions were consulted at the following libraries: Bibliothèque Nationale, Bibliothèque de l'Arsenal, Bibliothèque Sainte-Geneviève, Bibliothèque Mazarine. The 1560 edition is also found at the British Museum and the Thompson Memorial Library, Vassar College. An eighth edition of *Les Epistres*, referred to by Gustave Reynier as a Groulleau, 1550 edition of the *Oeuvres*, has not been located.

1. *Les epistres Famileres & inuectiues de ma dame Helisenne, composées par icelle dame, De Crenne.* Auec priuilege. Imprimées à Paris par Denys Ianot Libraire & Imprimeur, demourant en la rue neufue nostre Dame, à L'enseigne Sainct Iehan Baptiste pres Saincte Geneuiefue des Ardens (Privilege dated 18 October 1539, for three years). Paris: Denys Janot, 1539.

2. *Les œuures de ma dame Helisenne qu'elle a puis nagueres recogneues & mises en leur entier. Cest ascauoir les angoisses douloureuses qui procedent d'amours, Les Epistres familieres & inuectiues. Le songe de ladicte dame, le tout mieulx que par cy deuant redigées au vray, & imprimées nouuellemet par le commandement de ladicte Dame De Crenne.* On les vend a Paris en la grande salle du pallais au premier pillier, devant la chapelle de messieurs les

presidens, par Charles Langelier. 1543. Paris: Charles Langelier, 1543.

3. *Ibid.* Charles Langelier, 1544.

4. *Les Epistres famileres de ma dame Helisenne, de nouveau veues, corrigées oultre les precedentes Impressions. Les Epistres Invectives, de Madame Hélisenne, reueuës & corrigées de nouueau. Le Songe.* Paris: Estienne Groulleau, 1550. Text revised by Claude Colet, whose five-page letter, "A nobles et vertueuses Damoyselles . . . " is included as an appendix.

5. *Les œuvres de ma dame Helisenne de Crenne. A sçauoir, Les angoisses douloureuses qui procedent d'amours. Les Espistres familieres & Inuectives. Le songe de ladicte dame. Le tout reueu & corigé de nouueau par elle.* A Paris. On les vend en la grand'salle du Palais, au premier pillier, deuant la chappelle de messieurs les Presidens, par Charles l'Angelier. 1551. Paris: Charles Langelier, 1551.

6. *Les œuvres de ma dame Helisenne de Crenne. A sçauoir, Les angoisses douloureuses qui procedent d'amours. Les Epistres familieres & Inuectives. Le songe de ladicte dame. Le tout reueu & corige de nouueau par elle.* A Paris. Par Estienne Grouleau, demourant la rue neuue Nostre Dame à l'enseigne Sainct Iean Baptiste. 1553. Paris: Estienne Groulleau, 1553.

7. *Ibid.* Paris: Estienne Groulleau, 1560.

Modern Editions of Helisenne de Crenne's Works

Crenne, Hélisenne de. *Les Angoysses douloureuses qui procedent d'amours, Première partie.* Critical edition by Paule Demats. Paris: Les Belles Lettres, 1968.

———. *Les Angoysses douloureuses qui procedent d'amours, Première partie.* Edited by Jérôme Vercruysse. Paris: Lettres Modernes, 1968.

Secor, Harry. "Hélisenne de Crenne: *Les Angoysses doulou-reuses* (Part One)," Ph.D. dissertation, Yale University, 1957.

Critical Works on Helisenne de Crenne

Baker, M. J. "Fiammetta and the *Angoysses douloureuses qui procedent d'amours.*" *Symposium* 27, no. 4 (Winter 1973): 303–308.

———. "France's First Sentimental Novel and Novels of Chivalry." *Bibliothèque d'Humanisme et Renaissance* 36 (1974): 33–45.

Bergal, Irene. "Helisenne de Crenne: a Sixteenth-Century Novelist." Ph.D. dissertation, University of Minnesota, 1968.

Conley, Tom. "Feminism, *Ecriture*, and the Closed Room: the *Angoysses douloureuses qui procedent d'amours.*" *Symposium* 27, no. 4 (Winter 1973): 322–31.

Dusevel, Hyacinthe. *Biographie des hommes célèbres . . . du dé-partement de la Somme.* Amiens: Machart, 1835.

Dusevel, Hyacinthe. *Lettres sur le département de la Somme.* Amiens: Allo-Poiré, 1827.

Neubert, Fritz. "Antike und Christentum bei den ersten franzö-sischen Epistoliers der Renaissance, Hélisenne de Crenne und Estienne du Tronchet (1539 und 1569)." *Romanische Forschungen* 77 (1965): 1–41.

———. "Die französischen Briefschreiber der Renaissance und ihre Verleger." *Germanisch-Romanische Monatasschrift* 49, no. 18 (1968): 349–60.

———. "Hélisenne de Crenne (ca. 1500–ca. 1560) und ihr Werk. Nach den neuesten Forschungen." *Zeitschrift für Französische Spracho und Literatur* 80 (1970): 291–322.

Possenti, Antonio. "Hélisenne de Crenne nel secolo dei romantici e la prima conquista della critica." *Francia* 13 (January-March 1975): 27–40.

Saulnier, V.L. "Quelques nouveautés sur Hélisenne de Crenne." *Bulletin de l'Association G. Budé*, Quatrième Série, 4 (December 1964): 459–63.

Vercruysse, Jérôme. "Hélisenne de Crenne: notes biographiques." *Studi Francesi* 31 (January-April 1967): 77–81.

Waldstein, Helen. "Hélisenne de Crenne: a Woman of the Renaissance." Ph.D. dissertation, Wayne State University, 1964.

Medieval and Renaissance Works on Women

Agrippa, H. Cornelius. *De l'excellence et de la supériorité de la femme*. Translated by Roétitg. (First published as *De nobilitate et praecellentia foeminei sexus*. Antwerp: Michel Hillenius, 1529.) Paris: Imprimerie Delance, 1801.

———. *De l'Excellence et de la supériorité de la femme, ouvrage traduit du latin d'Agrippa, avec les commentaires de Roétitg* (François Peyrard). Paris: Louis, 1801.

Billion, François de. *Le fort inexpugnable de l'honneur du sexe féminin*. Paris: n.p., 1555.

Boccaccio, Giovanni. *Amorous Fiammetta*. Rarity Press, 1931.

———. *Flammette (de J. Boccace), complainte des tristes amours de Flammette à son amy Pamphile*. Lyon: Claude Nourry, 1532.

———. *Le Philocope [Filocolo] de messire Jehan Boccace, florentin, contenant l'histoire de Fleury et Blanchefleur, divisé en sept livres, traduitz d'italien en françoys par Adrian Sevin*. Paris: Denys Janot, 1542.

———. Boccace, Jean. *Le plaisant livre de noble homme Jehan Bocace, poète florentin, auquel il traicte des faictz et gestes des illustres et cleres dames, traduict de latin en françois*. Paris: Arnoul et Charles les Angelliers frères, 1538.

Caviceo, Giacomo. *Le Dialogue très élégant intitulé le Peregrin.* (Translated by François d'Assy.) Paris: A. Lotrian, 1531.

Champier, Symphorien. *La Nef des dames vertueuses, composée par maistre Simphorien Champier, docteur en médecine, contenant quatre livres: le premier est intitulé la fleur des dames; le second est du régime de mariage; le tiers est des prophéties des sibilles; et le quart est le livre de vraye amour.* Lyon: J. Arnollet, 1503.

DuPont, Gratien. *Les Controverses des sexes masculin et féménin . . . Requeste du sexe masculin, contre le sexe fémenin, à cause de celles et ceulx qui mesdisent de l'autheur du livre.* Paris: n.p., 1536.

Ficino, Marsiglio. *Discours de l'honneste amour sur le Banquet de Platon, par Marsile Ficin . . . traduit de toscan en françois par Guy Le Fèvre de la Boderie . . . avec un Traicté de I. Picus Mirandulus sur le mesme subject.* Paris: A. L'Angelier, 1588.

Flores, Juan de. *La Déplourable fin de Flammette, élégante invention de Jehan de Flores, espaignol, traduicte en langue françoyse [par Maurice Scève].* Paris: Denys Janot, 1536.

Héroët, Antoine. *Le Parfaicte amye.* Lyon: P. de Tours, 1542.

La Borderie, Bertrand de. *L'Amie de court inventée.* Paris: D. Janot et V. Sertenas, 1541.

Lefèvre (Fabri), Pierre. *Le Grand et vray art de pleine réthorique utile proffitable et necessaire a toutes gens qui desirent a bien elegantement parler et escripre.* Paris: Denys Janot, 1539.

Lemaire de Belges, Jean. *Les Illustrations de Gaule et singularitez de Troye, avec les deux Epistres de l'Amant vert.* Paris: François Regnault, 1528.

———. *Le Triumphe de l'Amant vert.* Paris: Denys Janot, 1535.

Machaut, Guillaume de. *Le Livre du voir-dit de Guillaume de Machaut, où sont contées les amours de Messire Guillaume de Machaut et de Peronelle dame d'Armentières, avec les lettres et les réponses, les ballades, lais et rondeaux dudit Guillaume et de ladite Peronnelle.* Paris: Société des bibliophiles françois, 1875.

Marot, Clément. *L'Adolescence clémentine, aultrement les Oeuvres de Clément Marot* [also contains a translation of the first book of Ovid's Metamorphoses]. Paris: Denys Janot, 1538.

————. *Colloque d'Erasme, traduict de latin en françois par Clément Marot, intitulé: Abbatis et eruditae.* Vander Haeghen: n.d. n.p.

Meung, Jean de. *Le Roman de la rose, par Guillaume de Lorris et Jean de Meung.* Ed. Ernest Langlois. Vol. I. Paris: Firmin-Didot, 1914.

Navarre, Marguerite de. *L'Heptaméron des nouvelles de très illustre et très excellente princesse Marguerite de Valois, royne de Navarre. . . .* Paris: J. Caveillier, 1559.

————. *Histoires des amans fortunez, dédiées à très illustre princesse Madame Marguerite de Bourbon. . . .* Paris: G. Gilles, 1558.

Orléans, Charles d'. *Poésies éditées par Pierre Champion. I. La Retenue d'amours. Ballades, chansons, complaintes et caroles.* Paris: H. Champion, 1923.

Pasquier, Etienne. *Lettres.* Paris: Langelier, 1586.

Pisan, Christine de. *Oeuvres poétiques de Christine de Pisan.* Edited by Maurice Roy. 3 vols. Paris: F. Didot, 1886–96.

————. *Le Trésor de la cité des dames . . . livre très utille et prouffitable pour l'introduction des roynes dames, princesses et autres femmes de tous estatz.* Paris: Denys Janot, 1536.

Pizan, Christine de. *The Book of the City of Ladies.* Translated by Earl Jeffrey Richards. Foreword by Marina Warner. London: Pan Books, 1983.

Tixier [also Textor], Jean. *De memorabilibus et claris mulieribus aliquot diversorum scriptorum opera.* Paris: Simon de Colines, 1521.

Other Works Consulted

Abensour, Léon. *La Femme et le Féminisme avant la Révolution.* Paris: Leroux, 1923.

Archambault, Paul. "The Ages of Man and the Ages of the World." *Etudes Augustiniennes* 11, no. 3–4 (Fall 1966): 193–224.

Augustin, Saint. *La cité de Dieu de saint Augustin, traduction de Raoul de Presles.* Abbeville: Jehan DuPré et Pierre Gérard, 1486.

———. *La Cité de Dieu: texte latin et traduction française.* 2 vols. Translated by Pierre de Labriolle (vol. 1) and Jacques Perret (vol. 2). Paris: Garnier, 1957–60.

Augustine, Saint. *The City of God against the Pagans.* Translated by George E. McCracken *et al.* The Loeb Classical Library. Cambridge, Mass.: Harvard University Press, 1963–72.

———. *Select Letters.* Translated by James Houston Baxter. The Loeb Classical Library. Cambridge, Mass.: Harvard University Press, 1930; rpt. 1965.

Bourrilly, V.-L. *Jacques Colin, abbé de Saint-Ambroise (14?–1547), contribution à l'histoire de l'humanisme sous le règne de François Ier.* Paris: Société nouvelle de librairie et d'édition, 1905; Geneva: Slatkine, 1970.

Cicero, Marcus T. *In Offi. Marci Tullii Ciceronis Officiorum libri tres, liber de Amicitia, liber de Senectute liber Paradoxorum. Opus Benedicti Brugnoli studio emaculatum . . . Desiderii Erasmi . . . hac editione suis locis additis.* Lyon: Gruphius, 1538.

Cicero, Marcus T.C. *De Oratore . . . Together with De Fato . . .* etc. Translated by H. Rackham. The Loeb Classical Library. Cambridge, Mass.: Harvard University Press, 1942; rpt. 1960.

Cicéron, Marcus T. *La première [et seconde] partie des Epistres familieres de M.T. Cicero, traduction française par Guillaume Michel, de Tours.* Paris: D. Janot, 1537–39.

————. *Les Oeuvres de M.T. Cicero . . . les Offices, le livre de l'Amitié, le livre de Vieillesse, les Paradoxes, le Songe de Scipio*. 2 vols. Paris: Denys Janot, 1539.

Etaples, Lefèvre d'. *La Sainte Bible en français*. Antwerp: n.p., 1530.

Fossier, Robert. *Histoire de la Picardie.*Toulouse: Private, 1974.

Froissart, Jean. *Poésies de J. Froissart, extraites de deux manuscrits de la Bibliothèque du Roi et publiées pour la première fois par J.A. Buchon*. Paris: Verdière, 1829.

Guénée, Bernard. *Le Métier d'historien au moyen âge*. Paris: Publications de la Sorbonne, 1977.

————. *L'Occident aux XIVe et XVe siècles*. Paris: P.U.F., 1971.

Herberay, Nicolas de. *Amadis de Gaule*. 5 vols. Paris: V. Sertenas, 1540–44.

Hicks, Eric. *Le Débat sur le roman de la rose*. Paris: Champion, 1977.

Jérôme, Saint. *Les Epistres monseigneur sainct Hierosme, en françois*. Paris: Guillaume Eustace, 1520.

Jerome, Saint. *Select Letters*. Translated by F.A. Wright. The Loeb Classical Library. Cambridge, Mass.: Harvard University Press, 1954.

Kany, Charles E. "The Beginnings of the Epistolary Novel in France, Italy, and Spain." University of California Publications in Modern Philology 21, No. 1: x, 1–158. Berkeley, Ca.: University of California Press, 1937.

Laertes, Diogenes. *Lives of Eminent Philosophers*. Translated by R.D. Hicks. Loeb Classical Library. Cambridge, Mass.: Harvard University Press, 1925; rpt. 1959.

Lille, Alain de [Alanus ab Insulis]. *Anticlaudianus. Patrologiae Cursus Completus Opera Omnia*. Edited by J.P. Migne. Paris: Petit-Montrouge, 1855, vol. 210, cols. 559–61.

Lorian, Alexandre. *Tendances stylistiques dans la prose narrative française du XVIe siècle*. Paris: Klincksieck, 1973.

Maclean, Ian. *Woman Triumphant: Feminism in French Literature 1610–1652.* Oxford: Clarendon Press, 1977.

Migne, J.P. *Patrologiae Cursus Completus.* 221 vols. Paris: Petit-Montrouge, 1844–64.

Omont, Henri. *Catalogue des éditions françaises de Denys Janot, libraire parisien (1529–1545).* Paris: Société de l'Histoire de Paris, 1899.

Ovidius Naso, Publius. *Les XXI épistres d'Ovide translatées de latin en françoys par monseigneur l'évesque de Angoulême* [Oct. de S. Gelais]. Paris: Galliot du Pré, 1528.

———. *Les XV livres de la Métamorphose d'Ovide . . . contenans l'Olympe des histoires poétiques . . .* Paris: Denys Janot, 1539.

———. *Metamorphoses.* Translated by Frank Justus Miller. 2 vols. London: W. Heinemann, 1916.

———. *Le Premier livre de la Métamorphose d'Ovide, translaté de latin en françois par Clément Marot . . .* Paris: Estienne Roffet, 1534.

———. *Le Recueil des epistres d'Ovide translaté en françoys o vray ligne pour ligne, faisans mencion de cinq loyalles amoureuses . . . c'est assavoir [V] Zénone pour Pâris, qui ravit Hélaine, [X] Adryane à Theseus, [VII] Dido à Enée, [II] Philis à Démophon et [VI] Ysiphile au vaillant Jason . . .* n.p. n.d., BN Res. Yc1567.

Plutarch. *Plutarque de Chéroné . . . traictant entièrement du gouvernement en mariage, nouvellement traduict de grec en latin et de latin en vulgaire françoys par maistre Jehan Lode.* Paris: Denys Janot, 1535.

———. *Plutarch's Lives in Eleven Volumes. VII. Demosthenes and Cicero, Alexander and Caesar.* Translated by Bernadotte Perrin. The Loeb Classical Library. Cambridge, Mass.: Harvard University Press, 1919; rpt. 1958.

———. *Les Vies des hommes illustres grecs et romains, comparées l'une avec l'autre par Plutarque, translatées de grec en françois* [par Jacques Amyot]. 2 vols. Paris: M. de Vascosan, 1559.

Quintilian. *Quintilien. Institution oratoire . . . Texte revu et traduit avec introduction et notes par Henri Bornecque*. 4 vols. Paris: Garnier, 1933–34.

Rawles, Stephen Philip John. "Denis Janot, Parisian Printer and Bookseller: A Bibliographical Study," Ph.D. thesis, University of Warwick, 1976.

Reynier, Gustave. *Le Roman sentimental avant l'Astrée*. Paris: Armand Colin, 1908.

Richardson, L. M. *The Forerunners of Feminism in the French Literature of the Renaissance*. Baltimore, London, and Paris: 1929.

Screech, M. A. *The Rabelaisian Marriage*. London: E. Arnold, 1958.

Telle, Emile-V. *L'oeuvre de Marguerite d'Angoulême, reine de Navarre, et la querelle des femmes*. Toulouse: Lion et fils, 1937.

Thomas Aquinas, Saint. *Summa theologica S. Thomae Aquinatis*. 8 vols. Paris: L. Vivès, 1856–60.

Vaganay, Hugues. *Amadis en français: Essai de bibliographie*. Florence: L. Olschki, 1906.

Versini, Laurent. *Le Roman épistolaire*. Paris: P.U.F., 1979.

Virgile, Publius V. Maro. *Enéide*. Translated by André Bellessort. Paris: "Les Belles Lettres," 1962.

———. *Les Enéydes de Virgille, translatez de Latin en françois, par messire Octavian de Sainct Gelais . . . revues et cottez par maistre Jehan de'Yvry*. Paris: A. Vérard, 1509.

Xenophon. *Xenophon in Seven Volumes. IV. Memorabilia and Oeconomicus*. Translated by E.C. Marchant; *Symposium and Apology*. Translated by O.J. Todd. The Loeb Classical Library. Cambridge, Mass.: Harvard University Press, 1923; rpt. 1968.

Zanta, Leontine. *La Renaissance du stoicisme au XVIe siècle*. Paris: E. Champion, 1914.

INDEX

A RENAISSANCE WOMAN

was composed in 11-point Mergenthaler Linotron 202 Sabon and leaded 2 points by
Eastern Graphics;
with display type in Libra by J. M. Bundscho, Inc.;
printed sheet-fed offset on 50-pound, acid-free Glatfelter Natural Hi Bulk,
Smyth-sewn and bound over 88-point binder's boards in Holliston Roxite C,
also adhesive bound with paper covers by Braun-Brumfield, Inc.;
with dust jackets and paper covers printed in 2 colors by Braun-Brunfield, Inc.;
and published by

SYRACUSE UNIVERSITY PRESS

SYRACUSE, NEW YORK 13244-5160